John M. Schwenzer (handwritten)
2007 (handwritten)

A Guide to the Architecture of St. Louis

A Guide to the

St. Louis Chapter, American Institute of Architects

Architecture of *St. Louis*

Introduction by George McCue

Text by Frank Peters and George McCue

Maps and Drawings by Pat Hays Baer

Project Coordinator, Doris Andrews Danna

Chair, AIA Guidebook Committee,
W. Philip Cotton, Jr.

University of Missouri Press

Columbia, 1989

Copyright © 1989 by
The Curators of the University of Missouri
University of Missouri Press, Columbia, Missouri 65211
Printed and bound in Japan

Library of Congress Cataloging-in-Publication Data
A Guide to the architecture of St. Louis / Introduction by George
McCue : Text by Frank Peters and George McCue : Pat Hays
Baer, maps and drawings.

     p.   cm.
   Includes index
   ISBN 0-8262-0679-4

  1. Architecture—Missouri—Saint Louis—Guide-books.
2. Saint Louis (Mo.)—Buildings, structures, etc.—Guide-books.
I. McCue, George.   II. American Institute of Architects. Saint
Louis Chapter.
NA735.S2P47 1989
720'.9778'66—dc19   88–9998
                                                    CIP

∞ This paper meets the minimum requirements of
the American National Standard for Permanence of Paper
for Printed Library Materials, Z39.48, 1984.

Contents

Acknowledgments

St. Louis has rich building traditions, and today it enjoys a promising civic vitality upon which to build for the future. The city's architecture mirrors development through growth, decline, and resurgence, in collective urban form as well as individual design examples.

The American Institute of Architects' St. Louis Chapter presents this guidebook with several purposes. It will help visitors and residents alike to discover new interest, meaning, and delight in our built environment. It is intended to be a special resource to those attending the AIA national convention here in 1989. And for those of us who may make decisions about the future of St. Louis architecture—what will be built, where, and how—a critical review of these examples will impress upon us our current responsibility to the city's culture and heritage.

This guide has been prepared by people who know St. Louis architecture well and have devoted much of their lives to its advancement. W. Philip Cotton, Jr., AIA, was largely responsible for planning the book's organization and content. He chaired the St. Louis Chapter's guidebook committee, which also included Betty Lou Custer, FAIA; H. Curtis Ittner, AIA; and Gerhardt Kramer, FAIA. Special credit is due to Doris Andrews Danna, AIA, who facilitated the entire editorial and production process as the committee's guidebook coordinator. It was a privilege to have the services of George McCue and Frank Peters, who have been respected commentators on St. Louis architecture for the *St. Louis Post-Dispatch*. Edward King and Jane Lago of the University of Missouri Press have been highly committed to this project and have provided generous assistance.

The present volume owes much to George McCue's *The Building Art in St. Louis*, an AIA-sponsored guidebook published in 1964, 1967, and 1981 editions. McCue's succinct and scrupulously researched material has, in many cases, been carried over unaltered into this guide. He has supplied a new general introduction to the present guide and has given valuable counsel in its preparation. All the photographs, drawings, and maps are new, and so are many of the entries, but this new AIA guide represents more a continuation of McCue's work than a departure from it.

Finally, we are grateful to the sponsors who generously supported the cost of preparing the new guide's contents. St. Louis is fortunate to have many dedicated friends of architecture among individuals, public agencies, businesses, trade organizations, and professional firms. Sponsorship opportunities were offered only after this volume's listings had been finalized by the St. Louis AIA Guidebook Committee; contributors to this project are listed on the following page.

American Institute of Architects / St. Louis Chapter
Clark S. Davis, AIA, President, 1988
Eugene J. Mackey III, AIA, President, 1989

Patrons

The American Institute of Architects
Anheuser-Busch Companies, Inc.
Associated General Contractors of
 St. Louis
Burks Associates, Architects
Betty Lou Custer, FAIA
Equitable Real Estate Investment
 Management, Inc.
Hastings & Chivetta Architects, Inc.
Hellmuth, Obata & Kassabaum, Inc.
Mr. & Mrs. H. Curtis Ittner
Ittner & Bowersox, Inc.
Kramer & Harms, Inc.
Kurt Landberg Architect, Inc.
Mackey Associates, P.C.
Maritz Inc.
Raymond E. Maritz & Sons, Inc.
 Architects
Masonry Institute of St. Louis
Monsanto Company
Murphy, Downey, Wofford &
 Richman, Inc.
Mysun Charitable Foundation
Nooney Company
Peckham Guyton Albers & Viets,
 Inc.
Pet, Incorporated
Powers Associates, Inc.
Ralston Purina Company
Rouse Missouri Management
 Corporation

Louis R. Saur & Associates, Inc.
Sheet Metal & Air Conditioning
 Contractors, St. Louis Chapter
SMP/Smith-Entzeroth
Southwestern Bell Foundation
Nolan L. Stinson, Jr., AIA Architect
Washington University School of
 Architecture
Wedemeyer Cernik Corrubia, Inc.

Special thanks to Mr. & Mrs.
 Vernon W. Piper for underwriting
 the cover and full-color section of
 this book.

Financial assistance provided by
The Saint Louis Regional Arts
 Commission

and The Missouri Arts Council.

Guide to the Guide

So many buildings, to be treated somehow in a little more than 200 pages: thoughtful readers are sure to raise objections. Why the Seib House on Lafayette Ave. but not the Helfenstein House in Webster Groves? Does Queeny Tower have something special that overshadows the larger, newer main pavilion of Barnes Hospital just to the east of Queeny? Is the little store building at Seventh and Olive, with its white terra-cotta ribbons, important enough to bump St. Louis Place, the big red office tower at 200 North Broadway?

Difficult choices had to be made, and a dozen editors would have made as many different selections. In any case, the purpose of this book is not to nail on the wall a list of blue-ribbon buildings. We hope readers will be stirred to look at the extraordinary architectural wealth around them, and to enjoy it without regard for either a qualitative hierarchy or questions of stylistic purity.

The book is organized into 13 geographic areas, starting Downtown and spreading outward to limits about 50 miles from the Gateway Arch. Each zone has one or two identifying initials (M for Midtown, NC for North County). The map on p. 28 shows zone boundaries, while the regional map on pp. 26–27 locates outlying towns.

Each section in the guidebook begins with a map of the zone to be dealt with. These area maps show the distribution of architectural examples within their boundaries. Each entry in the book has a locator tag in which the zone initial, or initials, is followed by a number: M12 is Midtown entry No. 12, Powell Symphony Hall.

Headings at each entry give the name and location of the building, its architect, and its date. These may not seem matters open to dispute, yet a building's authorship, construction, decoration, and revisions may sprawl messily over the annals of a century of more—assuming the annals haven't been thrown away.

Generally we have named the original architect of record, if one could be found, and omitted restoration and remodeling architects. Completion dates are preferred to cornerstone dates, present building names to old ones, yet we cannot claim either full success in the first matter or consistency in the second.

When a building is regularly kept open for visitors as a historic monument, we have indicated that. It was not so easy to deal with a rather large category of public or semi-public places—churches, schools, auditoriums, courts, office buildings—where casual entry has in recent years been made difficult or impossible for "security reasons."

Even addresses are not free from ambiguity. Southwestern Bell Corp. insists on One Bell Center as the address of its new headquarters tower, although the address of Bell's older downtown headquarters, in the next block west, is 1010 Pine St. To help visitors find One Bell Center, we have translated it as the 900 block of Pine St.

Many attractive walks will suggest themselves to readers as they follow the book. Still, nearly all will get to their starting point in some kind of vehicle, and they should equip themselves with good street or highway maps. Our maps are necessarily too small to substitute in that role.

Close observers may notice scattered discrepancies between some of our locality maps and what they see on the spot. That's because those maps were prepared from bases a decade or more old and do not register all the remodeling, demolition, and street alterations performed in the meantime. On some maps, significant buildings appear in black.

This book calls attention to homogeneous clusters of old buildings, or neighborhoods. Many of them, lacking individual monuments of high distinction, are nonetheless collective architectural experiences amounting to much more than the sum of their parts.

Trees, parked cars, close quarters, and lens distortion make these neighborhoods camera-resistant. To picture them we have used the kind of architectural drawing called a street elevation, in which rules of perspective are waived and each house in a row is seen head-on.

The effect is something like that of a walk down the street, with each house front examined successively. Don't take our word for it, though. See for yourself as you discover the fun of architectural touring in the St. Louis region.

St. Louis:
A City Discovering Itself

George McCue

St. Louis was founded as a French community under the Spanish crown. In its first years it was subject to attack by Indians instigated by the British, who were cut off from the fur trade west of the Mississippi by the strategic position of the new little settlement near the mouth of the Missouri River. The earliest structures were a stone warehouse, log houses, a log church, and hurried fortifications.

In its two and a quarter centuries St. Louis has availed itself of the abundant building materials of its region and responded with a variety of architectural means to the formative constraints and imperatives imposed by the natural environment.

The generally pleasant climate runs to occasional immoderate extremes. The recorded temperature range is 138 degrees, from 23 degrees below zero to 115 degrees above. High winds often inflict severe localized damage. Tornadoes of 1896, 1927, and 1959 tore out large areas of the city, and many subsequent buildings and reconstruction projects are monuments to those devastations.

Subterranean beds of quicksand are costly surprises. The Old Post Office (D29) rests on a 4-foot concrete slab poured atop 4,400 yellow pine piles driven through fluid sand, striking 11 springs. (Persistent legend has it that some 500 bales of cotton were packed between the piles, but research for the General Services Administration could not verify that.) The Railway Exchange Building, two blocks to the east, is supported by 110 concrete piers built to bedrock in pneumatic caissons. Excavators have broken through the ceilings of caves in the limestone that underlies much of the city. Old illustrations show South Side landscapes pitted with sinkholes caused by ancient subsidence, as in Carondelet Park today. Builders tried to avoid the caves, but some caves generated architecture by attracting breweries to build with access to constant cool temperatures for beer storage.

Small hills north and south of the early downtown proved to be Indian mounds containing burials and archaeological materi-

Landmark features of two centuries: First St., Laclede's Landing, in its original location and width as Grande Rue, 1764;
the Raeder Place building, right, in the iron facade construction that followed the riverfront fire of 1849; the Eads Bridge
ramp, crossing above the street, 1874; and the Gateway Arch,
completed in 1965.

als, and St. Louis was called the "Mound City" because of them.
One was hollowed out for brief use as a reservoir, but all were in
the way of subdivisions and all were destroyed. The belatedly
preserved Cahokia Mounds (I19) near Collinsville, Illinois, indi-
cate the extent of a veritable metropolis of Mississippian Indians.

The early builders found high-quality materials close by. Limestone could be pried from ledges in the riverfront bluffs and is
still quarried within the region. Forests of red cedar and fine
hardwoods bordered the village, and huge clay deposits came
into use for the brick, tile, and terra-cotta that gave St. Louis its
most characteristic building materials and its city blocks of ruddy
color. Outlying prairie land could be cultivated with minimum
clearance, and this was laid out in common fields that later became the sites of urban neighborhoods.

xiv

The Colonial Village

St. Louis was founded in 1764 by Pierre Laclede Liguest as a fur-trading post, but neither the French governor who granted the franchise nor the French traders who exercised it knew then that they were committing Spanish land. The city came into being as an outcome of a momentous confusion. After France lost Canada to the British and lost the Seven Years' War in Europe, it relinquished huge land holdings in the Mississippi Valley that it had controlled for a century. In payment for aid in the long war, and to frustrate the British, France transferred its land west of the Mississippi, and New Orleans, to Spain. The 1762 Treaty of Fontainebleau—instrument of the transfer—was kept secret because Spain was not then able to occupy the territory.

By the 1763 Treaty of Paris, France ceded all its land east of the Mississippi, except New Orleans, to Great Britain. Jean Jacques Blaise d'Abbadie was assigned to New Orleans as administrator to supervise the British transfer, but he was not informed until the next year of the Spanish transaction. Meanwhile, to revive business in the supposedly French domain of which he understood himself to be the governor, he granted trade monopolies in parts of the region. The firm of Maxent, Laclede and Company of New Orleans was awarded trade with Indians up to the present Minnesota River.

In August 1763 Laclede started up the Mississippi to Fort de Chartres (I28). He seems to have learned along the way that the east bank had become English, but he found the fort still in French hands. He established winter quarters there, then took his party on north to the Missouri River. Drifting back downstream, he stopped at the first elevated site on the west bank, where the Mississippi was overlooked by high limestone ledges. A sandy shore offered a landing place and a passage (later Market St.) up the slope. Laclede thereupon executed the first St. Louis land-use plan by notching some trees to mark building sites and streets, then returned to Fort de Chartres for the winter.

Construction was begun in the following February, when Auguste Chouteau, Laclede's stepson and at age 13 his lieutenant, returned to the site with 30 men to begin clearing. They erected log work huts and a one-story stone building, with a cellar dug by Indian women, for Laclede's trading post and residence. The next block was dedicated for a church and burying ground. The Old Cathedral (D7) stands there now.

A central public plaza was staked off in the block between Laclede's house and the river landing. Laclede recognized the potential of the village location at the center of a great river system for becoming "one of the finest cities in America." He named it for the crusader King Louis IX, patron saint of the royal house of France, and in the first year enticed some 40 families from the older villages of Cahokia and Kaskaskia across the river to leave English jurisdiction and again be part of a French community. Some removed their doors and windows for reinstallation at St. Louis.

Laclede's reports were lost, and it is still uncertain whether he knew or suspected by then that St. Louis belonged to Spain. (He learned it beyond a doubt in 1765 when his trade monopoly was canceled.) In any case the French regarded Spain as an ally. Charles E. Peterson, who did extensive research for the National Park Service, has pointed out that the village was planned in accordance with Spanish directives that had been standard since the 16th century for new settlements, and that the street widths and block dimensions in St. Louis corresponded to those prescriptions.

For five years the acting administrator of St. Louis was St. Ange de Bellerive, a Canadian officer who had turned Fort de Chartres over to the British in 1765 and was sent to St. Louis to perform a similar formality when the Spanish viceroy arrived. In 1770 the first Spanish lieutenant governor of Upper Louisiana, Don Pedro Piernas, took up his post as a renter of Laclede's house beside the plaza on the Rue de la Tour, now Walnut St. (Laclede died en route from New Orleans in 1778.)

Piernas acknowledged land grants issued by St. Ange, and he and his successors exercised benign authority. Spanish was the document language, but the spoken language and customs remained French. The four decades of Spanish jurisdiction left hardly a trace except in land grants that are the basis of titles to considerable city and outlying real estate. Spanish construction consisted of rudimentary fortifications. A large stone tower west of the church, at about the present site of Busch Stadium (D18), became the main element of a palisaded and trenched enclosure, Fort San Carlos, and later served as the city jail. Other defensive structures were built at the palisade corners, and their stones gradually found their way into other buildings and street paving.

Napoleon forced Spain to give up Louisiana in 1801; then, to finance his war with England, he sold the territory to the United States in the famous Louisiana Purchase of 1803. In a ceremony at St. Louis on 9 March 1804, the Spanish flag was lowered and the French flag raised to signify the transfer to France. The Fleur-de-lis was allowed to fly until the next morning by request of the villagers, then replaced by the Stars and Stripes.

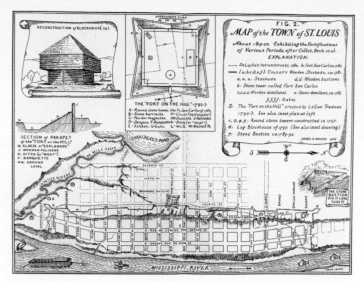

FIG. 2. MAP of the TOWN of ST. LOUIS. About 1819-20. Exhibiting the Fortifications of Various Periods, after Collot, Beck, et al.

A succession of Spanish lieutenant-governors built elements of the town fortifications as additions and replacements. In relation to present landmarks, the line extended along Fourth St. from four blocks south of the Poplar St. Bridge (Lombard St.) to the Martin Luther King, Jr., Bridge (Franklin Ave.).

Creole Construction

The village of 1804, as described by historian Frederic L. Billon, had "180 houses of stone and log, and a population not exceeding 1,000 souls." About one-fourth of the houses were stone, some laid up with mud for mortar, but the larger ones, with the principal story above a high basement or two full stories with attic, used cement made with lime burned in the village.

A few log houses had logs laid horizontally in the way of the traditional American cabin, but the preferred use of logs in the nearly square Creole houses was to set them on end, either in a backfilled trench (*poteaux en terre*) or, as may be seen in Cahokia's Holy Family Catholic Church (I20) and Creole Courthouse (I21), mortised into a sill on a stone foundation (*poteaux sur sole*). The upright logs were hewn square, channeled to receive filled-in stones and mortar, and spaced about one diameter apart. The walls were plastered and whitewashed inside and out, and the pristine whiteness of the village on its green hillside, with each lot marked off by its required palisade fence, was spoken of admiringly by visitors.

In form, the houses followed traditions of French Normandy and Quebec, with hip roofs originally made steep for thatching, and this pitch was retained when shingle or clapboard roofing

xvii

In old St. Louis, the stone house of Charles Gratiot, wealthy trader and landowner. The principal floor, above the full ground floor, looked out on a broad porch. The kitchen was in the lower wing for servants. Drawn by Clarence Hoblitzelle for proposed re-creation (not realized) of the original village for the Louisiana Purchase Exposition.

was used. But the hot summers of Louisiana and St. Louis made porches necessary for shade and to protect the plaster walls from rain. The break in the roofline where the lower pitch over the *galeries* at sides and ends met the steep pitch of the house roof produced the profile that distinguished a Creole house.

No colonial structure remains in St. Louis, but some can be viewed as restorations in Florissant (NC3) and Ste. Genevieve (OM8). The Menard House north of Chester, Illinois (I30), is a fine example of a large dwelling.

Creole Imprint on the Modern City

Laclede's village began fading after the first crude steamboat to visit St. Louis, the *Zebulon M. Pike* of Louisville, inaugurated regular runs in 1817. The riverfront became a panorama of warehouses and boat stores crowded along the old village slope to serve steamboats moored two and three deep along the levee. In 1849 the steamboat *White Cloud*, moored near the north end of the levee, caught fire. It was cut loose, but instead of drifting in the clear, it bumped along the line of boats, starting fires that destroyed 23 of them and 15 downtown blocks. The Old Cathedral was saved but little else.

The post-1849 buildings between the Eads (D3) and MacArthur bridges—the central part of the original village—were cleared for the Jefferson National Expansion Memorial and the Gateway Arch (D1), and all traces of streets were obliterated. The original street pattern and riverfront slope remain intact, however, in the

Creole construction of vertical logs with mud and rock infill in the Bienvenue House of 1786 on Third St. Logs were laid horizontally in the gables. Most of the early houses had interior chimneys. In this Hoblitzelle drawing the break in the roofline is apparent—steep near the peak, then eased outward over the porch, which did not extend around this house.

renovated blocks named Laclede's Landing (D5) just north of Eads Bridge. Some old streets also remain in blocks south of the Poplar St. Bridge (D9), but access is difficult.

In the downtown core east-west traffic now moves on extensions of Creole streets, and the form of today's St. Louis was significantly determined by the original town layout and its accretions of farmland.

It was from the boundaries of Creole common fields—strip plowlands extending westward from the village palisade along Fourth St.—that some streets, such as Kingshighway and Grand, inherited deflections from straightness. The strips were one arpent wide by 40 arpents long (about 192½ feet by 1½ miles), an arrangement that put farmers near enough together to hear warning shouts if Indians appeared. One strip was assigned for each town lot held and improved.

At the peak of this system, around 1790, the common fields had spread over five large tracts. First was the St. Louis Prairie, bounded by present Market, O'Fallon, and Fourth Sts. and Jefferson Ave. The dogleg on Jefferson north of Washington Ave. follows the boundary of that line of fields, which turned with a bend in the Mississippi River. The other common fields were Petite Prairie, Grand Prairie, Cul de Sac Prairie, and Prairie des Noyers. All the villagers shared another large tract, the St. Louis Commons, which extended more than seven miles south and

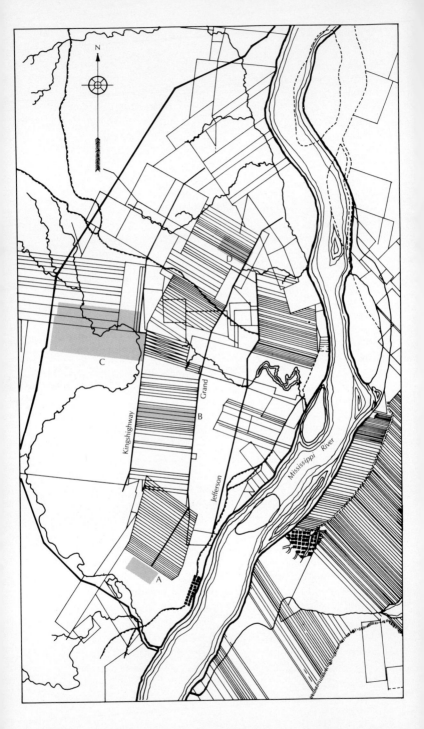

southwest to the River des Peres. It was fenced and used as a preserve for grazing and as a source of building timber and firewood. Strip farming, with the arduous labor of maintaining miles of wood fence, proved unwieldy. The Commons and common fields were divided into private land grants, then subdivided into the often erratic street patterns of jogs, dead ends, and skewed grids that baffle the sense of direction but give the older parts a certain charm. The only open land that remains of the Commons is the 30 acres of Lafayette Park, in Lafayette Square (NS12).

The American City

After the Louisiana Purchase, President Jefferson commissioned the Lewis and Clark exploration of the Missouri River—outfitted and concluded at St. Louis. The Missouri became the main avenue of Western commerce in furs and frontier commodities, and for years nearly everything and everybody going West or coming back passed through St. Louis, the hub of river transport and the marketing and provisioning point for the national expansion as symbolized by the Gateway Arch.

St. Louis was incorporated as a town in 1809 and as a city in 1822, the year after Missouri became a state. A gamut of social and political accommodations came into play as the 19th-century population was doubled and redoubled by arrivals from the eastern United States and by immigrants from troubled parts of central and eastern Europe.

The new nationals worked as laborers, established their own businesses and professions, made deep imprints on the cultural life, transplanted some homeland customs and animosities, and imparted a polyglot character to street sounds, place names, and local cuisine. The many construction artisans among them endowed their adopted city with streetscapes of Old World modes joined with American conventions and styles.

From a Catholic village where Protestant worship was prohibited, St. Louis became a predominantly Protestant city, and it absorbed a large and influential Jewish population. Church spires dominated the view above the low rooflines of both commercial buildings and houses, which rarely exceeded four stories. Mansions with facades of dressed sandstone were intermixed with rowhouses with parapeted end walls and coupled chimneys. Each chimney served its quota of heating and cooking stoves, all burning soft coal, and the sulfurous smoke accelerated flight to

Principal city parks in areas of the St. Louis common fields shown in relation to the tracts of strip farms. Bends in streets along common-field boundaries also can be seen here. A. Carondelet Park; B. Tower Grove Park; C. Forest Park; D. Fairgrounds Park.

Business and industry were mainly between Fourth St. and the river in this 1865 view past Lucas Place houses in foreground. Houses and churches predominate in the panorama. The dome of the then-new Old Courthouse is in the right background. Pointed corner towers identify the city's first high school building, by William Rumbold, designer of the Courthouse dome.

outlying areas. Numbers of splendid churches were abandoned within 20 or 30 years.

The 1849 fire and several cholera epidemics that caused thousands of deaths brought St. Louis to the realization that it was time to become a city in fact as well as in charter. Chouteau's Pond, once a clear lake southwest of the village, had become a dump for packinghouse offal and other filth. It was drained, and this flatland later became the railroad yards. Streets were made wider, and the first sewers constructed.

The architectural outcome of the fire was clean-slate reconstruction at the very time of the emergence of prefabricated cast-iron framing as support for wall enclosures. This technology did away with thick-walled, load-bearing masonry construction, gained interior space, and, as further developed in the steel skeleton and curtain wall, brought on the skyscraper. The visible signs in St. Louis of iron architecture's brief but exuberant existence were in facades related to classical orders and in ornament that rivaled the virtuosity of terra-cotta in invented designs. Good examples of ornamental iron details are in the 555 Washington Avenue building (D39), in the James Clemens, Jr., House (N1), and in Laclede's Landing, where the Raeder Place building (D6) with its 6-story iron front is a token of what had to be removed from some 40 homogeneous riverfront blocks to gain the Jefferson Memorial site.

In pre-elevator St. Louis, 1867, few business-district buildings exceeded four stories. What is now the Old Courthouse is at right, and the Old Cathedral spire projects above the skyline, center. Most other buildings in this view and beyond it to the right were demolished for the Jefferson National Expansion Memorial.

A Steel Bridge and Steel-Boned Buildings

The great years of the steamboat ended with the Civil War, although the most splendid craft were yet to come. The Eads Bridge (D3), completed in 1874, finished river transportation as a serious contender for freight and passenger service, for beneath its top deck for street traffic was a second deck with double railroad tracks—the linkage with eastern lines that had been cut off in East St. Louis. The tracks were run through a tunnel under Eighth St., to emerge in the new yards in the Chouteau's Pond basin.

A combine of St. Louis special interests representing steamboat lines, ferries, and steel fabricators had fought the Eads Bridge tooth and nail, and meantime four railroad bridges over the Mississippi upstream from St. Louis were decisive in shunting business into Chicago, which quickly overleaped St. Louis in population and importance to the mid-continent. St. Louis became the country's second-largest rail terminal, which it remains. The vast Romanesque Revival Union Station (D50), opened two decades after the bridge, stands as a monument to the prodigious railroad expansion, even though it no longer resounds to train-callers' announcements.

As a young architect in Chicago, Louis Sullivan had attentively followed reports in engineering journals of the innovative use of steel in the Eads Bridge construction. Twenty years later it was Sullivan and his partner Dankmar Adler who achieved the first realization of the skyscraper aesthetic in his steel-framed, 10-story Wainwright Building of 1892, with its tall brick piers and recessed spandrels proclaiming soaring, ground-saving tallness as an attribute of business buildings designed for cities. The tenant brochure emphasized a strong persuader: "elevators, four in number . . . of the best make . . . perfectly safe, and yet run at a high speed."

Electricity became available in St. Louis in 1884, and with it came the electric-powered elevator, which made tall buildings such as the Wainwright usable. Released from the limitation of rope-and-pulley and hydraulic elevators, downtown rooflines rose noticeably but not daringly. The tallest scraped the sky at around 8 to 12 stories—which was often the limit of smoke-obscured visibility anyway—until the Railway Exchange Building was pushed up to 21 stories in 1914 and Southwestern Bell (D23) to 26 in 1926.

Seventy-five buildings of more than five stories were built between 1887 and 1906, and they consistently reflected design disciplines of proportion, ornament, utility, and stately demeanor as instilled by the Ecole des Beaux Arts, Paris. Most of their architects had been trained in Paris; some had also been trained at Heidelberg, Rome, or London, or had received atelier tutelage from those professionals.

In the year of the Wainwright's completion, 1892, St. Louis building permits reached the peak of 5,500, involving about $20 million in construction costs along an estimated 39 miles of street frontage. Much of that frontage was along Washington Ave. (D35), where stores, warehouses, and loft factories built in that time remain as the last cohesive blocks of 19th-century commercial construction. Another remarkably homogeneous group is the Cupples Station ensemble (D22) built for warehousing and freight transfers at the edge of the railroad yards, near the end of the Eads Bridge tunnel. Originally 18 buildings but reduced in recent years for highway and stadium construction, the complex admitted lines of cars to basement platforms, from which hydraulic elevators hustled goods to work floors.

Exodus by Train and Streetcar

At first, technological advances—and particularly transportation, both vertical and horizontal—supported the traditional downtown concentration of goods and services for outlying residential neighborhoods, but eventually they would become instruments for the dispersal of both population and business centers.

In succession, the horse omnibus, horse rail cars, cable cars, electric streetcars, and the first motor buses made more parts of the city conveniently accessible, especially in a broad corridor running west and northwest from downtown that became the spine along which were distributed most of the major cultural activities—St. Louis and Washington universities, the symphony hall, fraternal organizations, libraries, and prime neighborhoods.

By 1881 nearly 120 miles of cable-car lines converging on the core extended north and south, and fanned out to Grand Ave. and Kingshighway. A narrow-gauge steam railroad ran between Grand Ave. and suburban Florissant, and two railroad companies ran commuter trains on their regular lines northward to Ferguson and southwest to Pacific via Webster Groves and Kirkwood (SC15). Fast interurban trolleys connected Ferguson and Kirkwood and took picnickers to Creve Coeur Lake. An Illinois electric interurban system with a large downtown terminal had cars and trains rocketing across the prairies to distant communities. City streetcar and bus lines, with connecting county buses, linked inner parts of the metropolis, and for modest fares one could travel from anywhere to anywhere on both sides of the river, give or take a few long waits at transfer points. The extraordinarily serviceable network remained in full use until after World War II.

Concentric movement inland from the river is an old story, for it was begun by the pioneers and accelerated by the cholera epidemics. Residents were repeatedly taken by surprise as the city expanded by leaps and bounds, with uninhibited invasions of residential blocks by factories, lumberyards, livery stables, and other such grossly mixed enterprises, causing the abandonment of schools and churches, and the conversion of houses to shops, saloons, and restaurants. When the Old Post Office site between Eighth and Ninth Sts. was determined in 1872, displacing residents as prominent as Wayman Crow, founder of Washington University, the location was lampooned in a *Puck* cartoon as closer to the Rocky Mountains than to the business center, then along Third and Fourth Sts. Dirt and noise sent households that could afford it out to the countryside for fresh air and yard space.

The Private Streets

In 1851 some well-to-do families built houses in Lucas Place, a street west of Missouri Park platted for private occupancy. (Now Locust St., west of Lucas Park; the Campbell House [D57] is the sole survivor.) This was the first of dozens of private streets or "places," established on high ground, that undertook to wall off encroachment with deed restrictions and covenants. Most of them followed established street grids, erected distinctive gateways, and set strict maintenance standards.

The most elaborate, off Union and Kingshighway north of Forest Park, became showcases of palatial eclectic design by the city's most prominent architects and by others of prestige from Boston, Chicago, and elsewhere, some of whom opened permanent St. Louis offices. Places of more modest inclination simply set out to become pleasant neighborhoods, but all were of distinctive quality.

xxv

There were European prototypes for the concept of the private place, but in St. Louis through the turn of the century (and later in some suburbs) it was applied to a unique extent. Most of the places remain, their amenities so persuasive that they have set examples for conversion by ordinance of some public streets to limited access as a means of stabilizing neighborhoods.

In the lurching kind of progress and retrogress that sometimes seems to characterize St. Louis, the city took two giant steps in 1876: it purchased more than a thousand acres of land out in the country for Forest Park, and through revision of the Missouri constitution separated itself from St. Louis County, thus becoming the state's only municipal county. Along with the latter action new city boundaries were established a few blocks beyond the western edge of the park site and in a long curve away from and back to the river north and south. Forest Park was a triumph of far-seeing vision, and the 1876 city limits an abysmal mistake.

In previous extensions of the city limits, more annexable territory lay beyond. This time trains made some of that open land temptingly visible, and electric streetcars were ready after 1887. Developers began organizing picnics and land sales in existing suburbs and in farmland subdivisions, with trolley lines either already in the area or quickly provided for new pockets of population.

In that hand-over-hand outward movement, affluent city families moved to big houses in Webster Groves, Kirkwood, Clayton, Normandy, Ferguson, Jennings, Florissant, and other village-like communities with garden space. Although low-interest, long-term financing had to wait for the Federal Housing Administration in the 1930s, families of limited income had good choices of small lots, where many moved into temporarily roofed basements and did their own construction as time and wages permitted.

Communities along the 1876 boundary qualified for charters of incorporation, and St. Louis was locked in. A hundred or so municipalities eventually dotted the map, with St. Louis County providing services to those not incorporated. There are erratic jurisdictions of street work, drainage, sanitation, and traffic control, and superimposed boundaries of school and voting districts, among other confusions of the Balkanized urban structure. Mayor-council power struggles are usually going on somewhere. A complex allocation of taxes collected and distributed by the county keeps it all running, and a proposal to join many small urban clusters into a few efficient big ones has met resistance: the de facto systems work well enough to cause misgivings that they might be made worse.

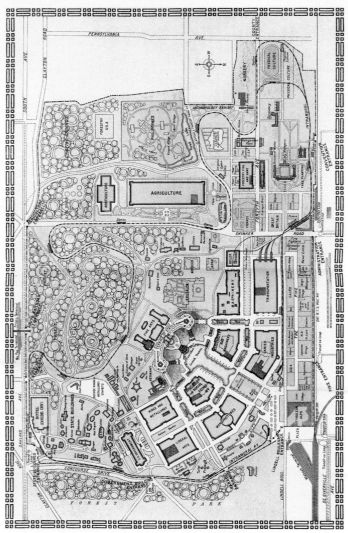

Formal quadrant of the Louisiana Purchase Exposition grounds, 1904.
Theme buildings and sculpture were in this area of grand design, and
the main entrance was off Lindell Blvd., lower right.

The Great Fair and Its Civic Impact

A St. Louis achievement that was magnificently right was the
1904 Louisiana Purchase Exposition, the biggest world's fair ever
staged, before or since. In an outpouring of creative energy, and
of excitement about the marvels that were emerging from the

smoking factories of the industrial age, the western part of Forest Park was cleared of ancient trees and transformed into a Beaux Arts panorama of vast exposition buildings disposed in a visionary cityscape of broad lagoons, cascades, and statuary. Except for the limestone Arts Palace, which remains as the St. Louis Art Museum (W35), the exposition "palaces" and their ornament, all intended to vanish after the fair, were finished in staff, a hard reinforced plaster. The inexpensive plasticity of staff made it the stuff of dreams, and it was cast into intricate fantasies of noble facades and sculptured allegories of peace and plenty that lived on in countless memories.

The fairs of that period generated City Beautiful visions that influenced American civic design for years to come, especially in ensemble rather than piecemeal conceptions of city centers. In 1907 the Civic League, a group of prominent citizens, architects, and landscape architects inspired by the fair of three years before, inaugurated comprehensive St. Louis city planning with publication of a report on the city's needs for new public works, private rehabilitation, and a coherent boulevard system. It delineated a downtown central parkway faced by government and quasi-public buildings and showed photographs of exemplary European streets juxtaposed with scenes of St. Louis dilapidation. Arguing for renewal of the city's historic ties with the river, the plan recommended shoreline improvements and, on the downtown frontage, a line of warehouses from the Eads Bridge to Poplar St. facing an esplanade built above a railyard of up to 20 tracks for freight and passengers, but predicated on electrification of locomotives "at no distant day."

In the next three decades riverfront schemes emerged repeatedly, all linking world's-fair ornateness with payback uses of disparate likelihood—office buildings, rail facilities, sports arenas, museums, airplane runways, and towers with dirigible rookeries. Tranquilizing porticoes and colonnades of white stone (the city's soot-laden air notwithstanding) framed plaza spaces of surreal incongruity with human scale, all to offset the envisioned high-density activities below decks. The common elements in these overdesigned conceptions were fixations on putting a white-city jacket over workshirt utility, and nonchalant attention to traffic circulation. They were duly noted in the Sunday rotogravures, but fortunately for the Gateway Arch they died aborning.

Rundown blocks downtown and deteriorating multiple-family dwellings in outer zones presented broader concerns than could be addressed with grandiose schemes for civic monuments. In 1911 the City Plan Commission, established by ordinance, initiated focus on basic improvements—streets and sewers, electric street lighting, parks, hospitals, and waterworks. The city's first zoning ordinance took effect in 1926, and for the first time surveys of housing conditions, welfare cases, and illiteracy, among other social and economic problems, were recognized as necessary to planned land uses.

In 1923 citizens passed a bond issue of $86 million, a national record, programmed for capital works divided between housekeeping and civic uplift. The latter included clearance for Memorial Plaza and construction of the Civil Courts Building (D14), Kiel Auditorium (D46), and the Soldiers' Memorial (D52). The United States Court and Custom House and the Post Office (D48) were built concurrently.

Memorial Plaza became the first section of an east-west mall, originally proposed in 1912 (the 1907 Civic League parkway was drawn north-south) to extend from Twelfth St. (now Tucker Blvd.) to Jefferson Ave. The west end was opened in successive clearances, with the fountain by Carl Milles, *Meeting of the Waters* (D51), its climax. The Gateway Arch became the east element, reinforcing the idea of the mall as a splendid urban axis. A national design competition was staged for the eastern blocks, but the unpopular winning scheme was discarded. After turbulent controversy the clearance and redevelopment proceeded with a combination of open space and blocks split between business towers and turf—the Gateway Mall (D12).

Urban Renewal

During the long Depression and World War II, construction was in abeyance throughout the aging inner city. Modest houses built to replace slum shanties of the early 19th century had gone full cycle, and the departed well-to-do had left acres of mansarded residences with parquetry floors and carriage houses to be garnered by absentee and straw-party owners for rent to the poor. These became low-maintenance 20th-century slums in which children woke up screaming with fingers and toes bleeding from rat bites.

The much-maligned urban renewal of the 1960s grew out of urgent needs for good housing and regained economic vitality in a city that, like others, had lost valuable assets to suburbia and was in serious overall disarray. From analysis of the levels of desperation a gamut of programs was devised focusing on what residents could do for their own houses and neighborhoods, and on what was required of the community in reutilizing blocks that were beyond salvage. Land for industrial and commercial uses was assembled through eminent domain procedures, and the dynamo that generated new construction was tax abatement.

Pruitt Homes of the Pruitt-Igoe project shortly after completion.

Developers wanted large tracts and maximum clearance, such as the 94 percent demolition of the 454 acres in Mill Creek Valley, east of Grand Ave. and south of Olive St. In what was sometimes called "Hiroshima Flats" the wide broom swept considerable property in decent condition out with the trash. A tornado forced what had been scheduled as gradual relocation of some of the city's poorest families, many of them previously displaced as southern sharecroppers, into an evacuation. Some doubled up in what had been stable black neighborhoods, and others flooded new public housing, with a heavy influx in two big projects, Pruitt and Igoe, in the near North Side.

These became merged as Pruitt-Igoe—33 slab towers, each 11 stories, completed in 1955 and built in staggered alignment along former streets so that they could plug into existing utility lines. Put up with remarkable economy to meet budgets cut back by federal specifications, they had reduced costs by omitting ground-floor toilets that would have served playgrounds, by providing elevator stops only at floors four, seven, and ten, and by using much light, unpainted construction that later needed costly maintenance. Widely acclaimed at first for architectural response to urgent social needs, Pruitt-Igoe and its urine-soaked elevators became, within two decades, the most notorious disaster in public housing. Books and research archives are filled with reasons. All the buildings were demolished by implosion in 1973, and the site is another clean slate.

Pruitt-Igoe reduced to rubble, with a twisted reinforcing bar in grotesque resemblance to the form of the distant Gateway Arch.

Here, Now, and Beyond

It is well established that the flight to suburbia was highly motivated by a yearning to have it both ways: a simpler life with the familiar village symbols of broad yards, gardens, fresh air, front porches, and shared values, but keeping easy access to the amenities of the city left behind. Something like the ideals of the Creole village but with modern conveniences and no need for fortifications.

Where it is still working it works well, but the problems left behind are following their own invasion channels into the good life. Private-place residents walled them off, and suburban settlers moved away from them, but now some of the deep-rooted predicaments of cities are being confronted and persistently dealt with, even at great expense in courage and money.

The city is looking good again as a dwelling place, and the wealth of well-built older housing stock in St. Louis offers challenging opportunities for regaining in-town amenities through use of that potent new/old tool, sweat equity. With goading and practical guidance from the Landmarks Association of St. Louis, the city became the national leader in adaptive reuse of houses and commercial buildings that a few years ago would have been absentmindedly scraped away.

The move back from the suburbs into reclaimed houses has been called gentrification and has been charged with depriving poor families of last-stage shelter that had been their main recourse outside the projects. The abjectness of the concept of reserving houses in ruinous condition for the poor suggests the poverty of ideas in this area of urgent concern.

Architecture has generated good social conditions by giving them good growing environments, and it has exacerbated some conditions that were actually beyond the scope of architecture and were clearly marked for the attention of all citizens. Urban-studies programs in secondary schools might help eventually to develop what every architect needs, the enlightened client.

Gateway Arch (see D1, p. 31) and Old Courthouse (D11, p. 36).

Color Photographs

The color illustrations, for the most part, are arranged in chronological order by date of building completion. Further information concerning the structures illustrated here can be found in entries in the appropriate geographical sections; the entry numbers are designated in the captions.

1

Archambault House (see NC4, p. 157)

Eads Bridge (see D3, p. 32)

2

Campbell House interior (see D57, p. 59)

Dovecot Picnic Pavilion, Tower Grove Park (see S15, p. 109)

3

Bissell St. Water Tower
(see N8, p. 118)

Grand Ave. Water Tower
(see N7, p. 118)

4

Compton Hill Water Tower (see NS18, p. 98)

5

Wainwright Building (see D24, p. 42)

Wainwright Building, window detail

Wainwright Building, cornice detail

Wainwright Tomb, Bellefontaine Cemetery (see N13, p. 120)

7

Anheuser-Busch Brew House interior (see NS7, p. 94)

Union Station interior (see D50, p. 54)

Overleaf: Union Station at night

8

Washington Terrace gate (see W26, p. 79)

St. Francis de Sales Church interior (see NS17, p. 98)

12

Ridgley Hall, Washington University (see UC6, p. 127)

Cathedral of St. Louis interior (the "New Cathedral"; see W5, p. 71)

13

Soldan High School (see W31, p. 81)

Vernacular houses from the 7900 block of Michigan Ave. (see "Some Old Vernacular House Types")

14

Four vernacular house types: a mansarded brick flat (top left), a two-family house (top right), a town-house (right), and a North Side group exemplifying quality in construction and pride in maintenance (center).

15

Powell Symphony Hall interior (see M12, p. 67)

Fox Theater interior (see M9, p. 65)

16

Howard House, Principia College (see I4, p. 179)

Milles Fountain (see D51, p. 56)

Pappas House (see WC11, p. 140)

Climatron, Missouri Botanical Garden (see S5, p. 104)

Priory Chapel interior (see WC12, p. 140)

18

Mallinckrodt Corporate Center (see NC10, p. 159)

General American National Service Center (see SC20, p. 153)

McDonnell Douglas Information Services Co. (formerly McDonnell Automation Co., "McAuto") (see NC11, p. 159)

20

Citicorp Mortgage Inc., St. Louis headquarters (see WC14, p. 141)

Edison Brothers Distribution Center (see D49, p. 54)

21

1010 Market St. (see D17, p. 39)

Herman Stemme Office
Park, Building No. 1
(see WC16, p. 142)

22

St. Louis Centre (see D37, p. 49)

23

MCI Building (see D19, p. 39)

A Guide to the Architecture of St. Louis

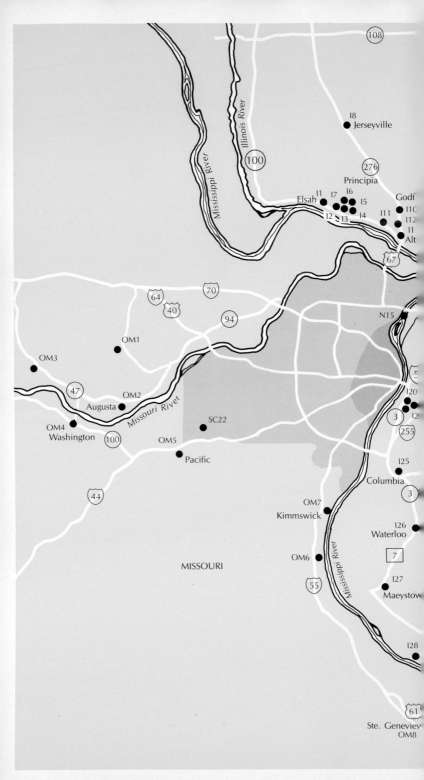

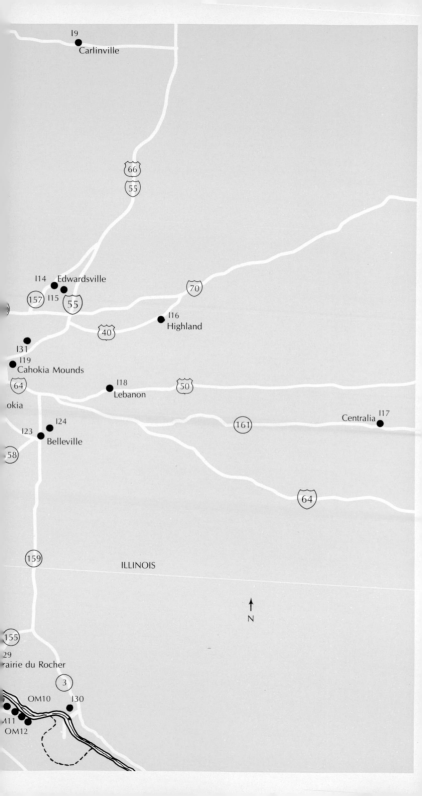

I9 Carlinville

66 55

I14 Edwardsville
157 I15 55

70

I16 Highland

40

I31

I19 Cahokia Mounds

64

okia

I18 Lebanon

50

I24
I23 Belleville

161

Centralia I17

58

64

159

ILLINOIS

↑
N

155

29
Prairie du Rocher

3

OM10 I30

M11
OM12

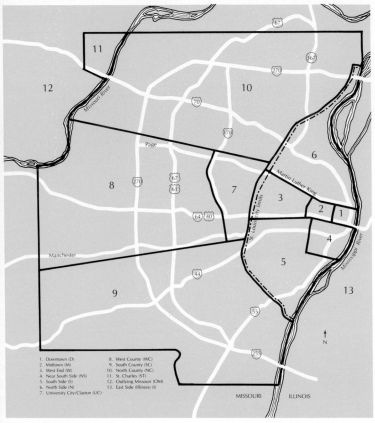

1. Downtown (D)
2. Midtown (M)
3. West End (W)
4. Near South Side (NS)
5. South Side (S)
6. North Side (N)
7. University City/Clayton (UC)

8. West County (WC)
9. South County (SC)
10. North County (NC)
11. St. Charles (ST)
12. Outlying Missouri (OM)
13. East Side (Illinois) (I)

Key to Area Maps

1. Downtown (D)
2. Midtown (M)
3. West End (W)
4. Near South Side (NS)
5. South Side (S)
6. North Side (N)
7. University City/Clayton (UC)

8. West County (WC)
9. South County (SC)
10. North County (NC)
11. St. Charles (ST)
12. Outlying Missouri (OM)
13. East Side (Illinois) (I)

28

1 Downtown

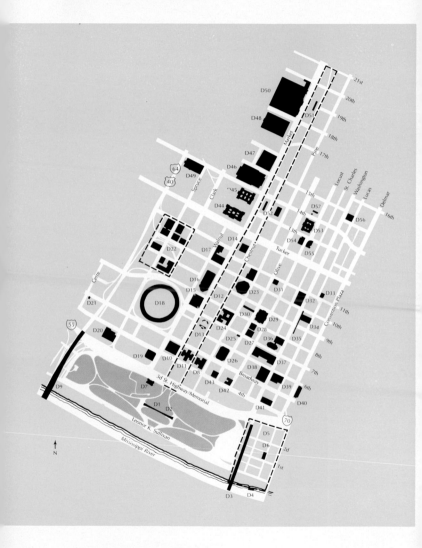

St. Louis celebrated its bicentenary in 1964, but no first-generation or second-generation buildings remain from the little French post on the bank of the Mississippi. The oldest within the downtown district is the Basilica of St. Louis or "Old Cathedral," erected in 1834 (see D7).

As the Old Cathedral went up, St. Louis entered a period of very rapid growth, changing in little more than a decade from a village into a metropolis. The population increased tenfold between 1840 and 1860 and nearly doubled in the ten years after that. By 1870 St. Louis had 310,864 residents and was the nation's fourth city.

Such pell-mell expansion brought close-order cycles of building and demolition in the area now thought of as Downtown. Residences succumbed to churches, shops gave way to hotels, office buildings to banks, brokerages to warehouses. Everybody kept moving west.

The pace of growth moderated after 1870. That is why so much of what you see in Downtown dates from the last third of the 19th century and the first third of the 20th. The Depression, World War II, and a long period of postwar uncertainty saw little new Downtown construction; revival came only with the 1960s. Most of the energy of civic leadership in the period from 1930 to 1960 was bent on demolition, to create parking for cars, ornamental plazas for pedestrians, vacant land for redevelopers, and public-housing towers in place of what were habitually called tenements and slums.

Two walks are recommended for those who want to see St. Louis's proud, robust old commercial buildings in homogeneous groups, with relatively few gaps from demolition. One is around the little district called Laclede's Landing (see D5), just north of the Eads Bridge approach, the other along Washington Ave. from Eads Bridge west to Fifteenth St. (see D35).

D1. Gateway Arch, Jefferson National Expansion Memorial

Downtown riverfront; Eero Saarinen & Associates, 1965

Intended as a monument to St. Louis's role as gateway to Western expansion following the Louisiana Purchase, the Arch has become a unique symbol of the city itself. It is 630 feet high and 630 feet wide at the base, in section an equilateral triangle whose sides narrow from 51 feet at ground level to 17 feet at the top. The profile is usually called a catenary curve, defined by a hanging loop of chain, but to Saarinen that curve looked too pointed. To flatten and spread the catenary form as he wished, Saarinen's engineers devised an imaginary chain, shaped like the Arch itself—three times thicker at the ends than at the apex.

The visible stainless-steel skin is ¼ inch thick. It and an inner wall of steel plate ⅜ inch thick are the chief structural members of the Arch. The space between the two steel walls is filled, up to the 300-foot level, with post-tensioned concrete rooted deep in the earth. Steel stiffeners connect the walls the rest of the way up. This elaborate structural system left room inside, as Saarinen wished, for cable cars to take visitors to an observation platform in the top of the Arch.

Planning was begun in 1933 to clear the 19th-century buildings from the site of Laclede's settlement and to raise on it a park or monument commemorating the opening of the West. Saarinen's design won a national competition in 1948. He did not live to see his Arch begin to rise 15 years later.

See also color photograph, p. 1.

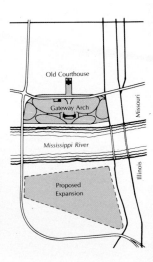

31

D2. Museum of Westward Expansion

Downtown riverfront; Aram Mardirosian, 1976

When the Gateway Arch rose in the middle 1960s, below-grade space at its feet was enclosed for a museum and two theaters. This area, nearly as large as a football field, remained a roughed-in void for a decade. The museum sets forth the drama of Western emigration in terms of the people who went West, their tools, their personal belongings, and their interpretations of what was happening.

D3. Eads Bridge

Foot of Washington Ave.; James Buchanan Eads, 1874

It was a pioneering bridge in several engineering respects, and it remains a beautiful one, with its studied proportions and its balance of steel with masonry. For St. Louis's first Mississippi River bridge Eads chose to use chrome steel, a metal still in the development stage; he designed the world's first steel truss spans, and to sink piers in the riverbed used pneumatic caissons for the first time in the United States. He also found a way to build tubular-steel arched spans without falsework giving support from below—he extended them outward in both directions from the two deep-water piers so that the lengthening wings of steel remained in balance.

A double track, out of service since 1974, carried rail traffic from the east into a tunnel under Washington Ave. The 54-foot-wide top deck of the bridge still carries vehicular traffic. The center span of 520 feet is flanked by spans of 502 feet; the whole bridge, counting the long Illinois approach, is 6,220 feet long.

See also color photograph, pp. 2–3.

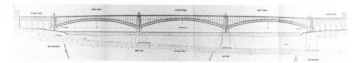

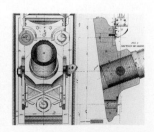

32

D4. Goldenrod Showboat

Downtown riverfront; Capt. W. R. Markle, 1909

This largest of showboats toured river towns before mooring permanently in St. Louis in 1937. Its wooden superstructure now rests on a steel hull.

D5. Laclede's Landing

A few blocks of 19th-century commercial, industrial, and storage buildings survive along streets that were laid out in St. Louis's first generation of activity as a riverside trading post. Hundreds like them on the south side of the Eads Bridge approach were demolished to make room for the Jefferson National Expansion Memorial (see D1). Restoration and development in recent years gave this old district the name Laclede's Landing.

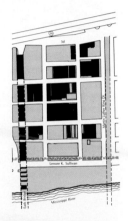

33

D6. Raeder Place

727 North First St.; Frederick William Raeder, 1874; remodeling by Kimble A. Cohn & Associates, 1980

A former tobacco factory with a six-story cast-iron facade of exceptional quality, one of the sights of Laclede's Landing (see D5). It has been converted into luxurious offices with retail shops and restaurants on the ground floor and in the basement.

D7. Basilica of St. Louis, King of France (Old Cathedral)

Walnut St. east of I-70; Joseph C. Laveille and George Morton, 1834; renovation by Murphy & Mackey, 1963

The oldest cathedral west of the Mississippi stands on the only privately owned ground in the Jefferson Memorial area. The site was reserved for church use in 1764 by Pierre Laclede Liguest and is owned by the St. Louis Archdiocese. This stone building with Doric portico and 135-foot spire was the fourth church to rise on the site.

D8. Boatmen's Tower

100 North Broadway; Hellmuth, Obata & Kassabaum, 1976

A 22-story office tower in the block north of the Old Courthouse takes respectful notice of the older building by approaching it with a much lower enclosure that serves as the Boatmen's Bank lobby. The lobby's skylighted space-frame roof and landscaped entrance plazas further temper the severity of the aluminum-and-glass tower.

D9. Poplar St. Bridge

Foot of Poplar St.; Sverdrup & Parcel and Associates, 1967

To carry interstate highway traffic over the Mississippi, engineers sought a design in harmony with the grace of Eads Bridge and the Gateway Arch, without a superstructure that would obtrude on highway travelers' view of the city. The answer was a new kind of bridge called orthotropic, in which plate-girder spans are made exceptionally long and slender by being united structurally with a traffic-carrying deck of steel. This, the first such bridge in the United States, crosses the river in five spans, of which the longest is 600 feet. Orthotropic bridges were pioneered in Germany; one of the Rhine bridges, at Cologne, that served as a model for Sverdrup engineers is shown in the lower photograph.

D10. Equitable Building

10 South Broadway; Hellmuth, Obata & Kassabaum, 1971

This 21-story office tower clad in reflective glass stands on the block directly south of the Old Courthouse. It and Boatmen's Tower (D8) were designed by the same architects with the same care for framing the 19th-century monument in a hospitable, symmetrical composition. As does the lobby of Boatmen's Tower, Equitable's two-story northern bay, containing retail shops, approaches the Old Courthouse deferentially.

35

D11. Old Courthouse

Broadway and Chestnut, Market and Fourth Sts.; Henry Singleton, 1839–1845; Robert S. Mitchell, 1852–1862; William Rumbold, 1860–1864

Singleton added extensively to an 1820s courthouse on the site, retaining it as the east wing of a cruciform building in Greek Revival style, with a low cupola over the central rotunda. Mitchell demolished the old east wing, remodeled Singleton's west wing, and added large annexes at the south and north ends of the 1839–1845 building, keeping as he did the Greek Revival manner established by Singleton. Rumbold substituted an Italian Renaissance dome for Singleton's low cupola. It is a precursor of the cast-iron dome placed on the United States Capitol in Washington during the Civil War. The strength of Rumbold's novel design was suspect, but he proved it by loading a model of the new dome with 6½ tons of pig iron. See also color photograph, p. 1.

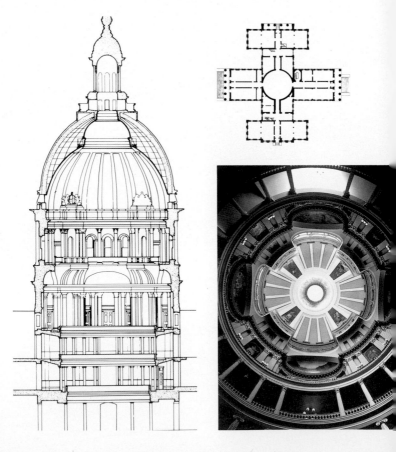

D12. Gateway Mall

The idea of clearing away buildings between Market and Chestnut Sts. for a monumental promenade or plaza is an old one. The strip in question extends from the riverfront to Twentieth St., and in fact few buildings remain in the strip between the Gateway Arch and Aloe Plaza in front of Union Station. Irregular street alignment, however, and sharp differences in elevation from one end to the other have discouraged efforts to unify the strip in one long prospect. A large and distinctive public building, the Civil Courts (D14), interrupts the vista between Eleventh St. and Tucker Blvd., while a modern 19-story office building at 1 South Memorial Drive blocks the Mall stroller's view of the south leg of the Arch. A great deal of acrimony has attended every act of construction and demolition in the Mall strip. Even the Old Courthouse was threatened by wholesale clearance near the riverfront in the 1930s. It lived to become a key in the Mall lineup, but recent above-grade constructions for the Morton D. May Amphitheater (D13) interfere with the view of the Old Courthouse from points west. A large office building, One Gateway Mall, has risen within the same Mall precinct that was assiduously cleared of older office buildings. The Gateway Mall addition more rancorously discussed than any other, however, is Richard Serra's relatively inconspicuous 1983 sculpture *Twain*, an arrangement of upright slabs of two-inch-thick Cor-Ten steel in the block between Tenth and Eleventh Sts.

A. Aloe Plaza; B. Milles Fountain; C. Civil Courts; D. Serra Sculpture *Twain*; E. One Gateway Mall; F. Morton D. May Amphitheater; G. Kiener Plaza; H. Old Courthouse

D13. Morton D. May Amphitheater

Gateway Mall, east of Seventh St.; Team Four Design, 1987

A stepped, marble-lined pit of irregular contour with cascading water, and with Postmodern pavilions and pergolas at street level, was laid out to animate the Mall for strollers.

37

D14. Civil Courts

Tucker Blvd., Eleventh, Market, and Chestnut Sts.; Klipstein & Rathmann, 1930

Nobody knows the exact appearance of the famous tomb that King Mausolus of Caria built for himself at Halicarnassus, but it was probably tall with a pyramid on top, and so is St. Louis's Civil Courts building. The room behind the colonnade just below the pyramid houses a law library that, with its height, airiness, light, and good proportions, constitutes an unusual and attractive interior space.

D15. General American Life national headquarters

Market, Walnut, Seventh, and Eighth Sts.; Philip Johnson and John Burgee, 1977

A three-story square building is divided diagonally like a sandwich, and one of the halves raised to six-story height, with ten columns inserted to hold it aloft. A cylindrical rotunda runs up through the center, serving both halves with glass-walled elevators.

D16. Centerre Bank Building

Market, Walnut, Eighth, and Tenth Sts.; 3D/International Consultants, 1981

A 31-story shaft, turned 45 degrees to the street grid, is beveled at the corners to make the plan octagonal; a 3-story extension extends west on the two-block site. A dark, sleek specimen of the corporate-tower genre.

38

D17. 1010 Market St.

Market, Walnut, Tenth, and Eleventh Sts.; Edward Larrabee Barnes, 1981

This 20-story tower, elegant in its proportions and crisply detailed, rose in the 1980s but constitutes downtown St. Louis's nearest approach to classic International Style. See color photograph, p. 22.

D18. Busch Stadium

Broadway and Seventh, Walnut and Spruce Sts.; Sverdrup & Parcel and Associates, 1966; Edward Durell Stone, design collaborator; Schwarz & Van Hoefen, associated

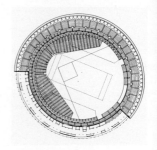

Nearly circular arena has seats for 50,222 at Cardinal baseball games, none with an obstructed view. The stadium profile is low because the playing field and some seats are below grade. The crowning thin-shell canopy projects inward 70 feet above the top tiers of seats.

D19. MCI Building

100 South Fourth St.; Hellmuth, Obata & Kassabaum, 1987

Twelve stories and 278,700 square feet, wrapped in reflective glass of a pleasant grass-green tint. The plan is a rectangle with the southeast and northwest corners rounded into broad quarter-cylinders. At the south end, the office building straddles two-story cabana units of the neighboring Clarion Hotel, which sold air rights to the developers. See color photograph, p. 24.

D20. Pet, Inc. headquarters

400 South Fourth St.;
A. L. Aydelott, 1969

The "New Brutalist" style challenged sheer curtain-wall construction with dramatically sculptured lines, high relief, and relatively small windows cut into expanses of concrete. The major influence was late work by Le Corbusier, in particular his government buildings at Chandigarh, India.

D21. Eugene Field House

634 South Broadway; c. 1845

Childhood home until 1856 of the poet and journalist who wrote "Little Boy Blue" and other popular short pieces. Most of the furnishings are from Field's Chicago home. This was one of a row of 12 similar houses, saved when the others were demolished in 1936.

D22. Cupples Station

Seventh, Eleventh, Spruce, and Poplar Sts.; Eames & Young, 1892

These buildings (at right) remain of 18 that formed a freight-handling, transfer, and storage complex near the mouth of the mile-long double-track tunnel leading from Eads Bridge to the railyards of Mill Creek Valley. The buildings differed in decorative detail and fenestration but were successfully designed to harmonize in scale, and those that remain constitute a noble group.

40

D23. Southwestern Bell buildings

1010 Pine St.; Mauran, Russell & Crowell, 1926
900 block of Pine St.; Hellmuth, Obata & Kassabaum, 1986

The older Bell headquarters tower has setbacks, vertical ribs, and finials for a skyscraper-Gothic effect. The recent tower to the east, named One Bell Center, has walls of sheer polished granite and glass most of the way up, with notching and setbacks near the top that recall 1930s skyscraper profiles. One Bell Center is a grand and solemn addition to the skyline, and its precisely aligned granite cladding responds with interesting variety to changes of light and weather.

41

D24. Wainwright Building

709 Chestnut St.; Adler & Sullivan, Charles K. Ramsey, 1892

The spirit of the modern skyscraper was discovered in the Wainwright Building, the first architectural break from thick-walled load-bearing masonry, and from earlier Chicago and New York buildings framed in metal but preserving the look of masonry construction. The Wainwright, in the words of Frank Lloyd Wright, is a monument to the first perception of "the tall building as a harmonious unit—its height triumphant." In some respects it is a transition, for the steel frame rises through only every second column, and the cornice remains, like the capital of a column in which the first two stories are the base, the next seven the shaft. The setback windows are alternated with terra-cotta panels ornamented with relief designs, varied at each floor. The attic story is an elaborate frieze of intertwined leaf scrolls and circular windows. See also color photographs, pp. 6–7.

Wainwright State Office Building

Seventh, Eighth, Chestnut, and Pine Sts.; Hastings & Chivetta, renovation, with Mitchell/Giurgola, additional buildings, 1981; program and interior design by Team Four Design

The Wainwright and the rest of its block were purchased by the state government of Missouri for an office complex, with the plan chosen by competition. Three L-shaped buildings frame a drive-in entrance, an inner court, and a fountain court on Chestnut St. The Wainwright elevators were moved to an added rear shaft to serve all the buildings, and the light well became an atrium lobby with a bridge on each floor.

D25. 224 North Seventh St.

Southeast corner of Seventh and Olive Sts.; Louis Curtiss, 1910

A rococo confection in white terra-cotta nestles demurely among some of the city's grandest and heaviest buildings—one narrow bay five stories high aflutter with divinity ribbons and medallions. Curtiss was a talented Kansas City architect.

D26. Metropolitan Square

Broadway and Sixth, Pine and Olive Sts.; Hellmuth, Obata & Kassabaum, 1988

A 42-story office tower with granite-and-glass curtain wall and Postmodern decoration in the form of steep roof gables and bay-window stacks. Rich polychrome marble veneer in a large lobby, with murals by Lincoln Perry and Terry Schoonhoven. The building is 600 feet tall, 20 feet higher than Southwestern Bell's One Bell Center (D23) and 30 feet lower than the top of the Gateway Arch.

D27. 705 Olive St.

Northwest corner Olive and Seventh Sts.; Adler & Sullivan, Charles K. Ramsey, 1893

Built soon after the Wainwright as the Union Trust Building and more purely expressive of its structure, since each pier contains a steel supporting column. This photograph shows Union Trust before a 1924 remodeling removed the Roman-arched entrance, the row of big round second-story windows, and rampant lions at the corners. Some of the round windows survive facing the alley to the west of the building. The detail photograph shows a terra-cotta lion's head from the colonnade at the top of Union Trust. The remodeled building appears to the right of the Chemical Building in photograph with the following entry.

D28. Chemical Building

Northeast corner of Olive and Eighth Sts.; Henry Ives Cobb, 1896; Mauran, Russell & Garden, addition, 1902

Some of the last cast-iron ornament to be installed in St. Louis is in these crisply articulated facades of brick with terra-cotta trim. The exterior, with exactly matching addition (both to the left in the photograph), is closely related to Chicago's vanished Tacoma Building, by Holabird & Roche, in its exposure of windows in stacked oriels.

45

D29. Old Post Office

Olive, Locust, Eighth, and Ninth Sts.; Alfred B. Mullett, 1873–1884; Patty, Berkabile, Nelson/Harry Weese, restoration and remodeling, 1982

Built as a federal court and custom house. Mullett's massive Second Empire structure is made more fortresslike by the granite facing, by a 25-foot-deep moat at sidewalk level to let light into two basements, and by deep-set windows over which thick steel shutters can be drawn for fire protection. The sculptural group high on the Olive St. front, where a 67-foot iron-framed mansard cupola crowns the building, is by Daniel Chester French.

Repeated efforts to have the government tear down the Old Post Office, in favor of a parking garage or a larger federal office building, were finally thwarted with passage by Congress of a bill encouraging shared federal occupancy of the historic building. Federal offices and agencies are now on the upper three floors, while the main floor and two basement levels are reserved for commercial mall use.

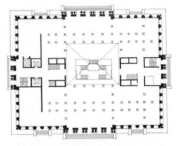

46

D30. Arcade Building

812 Olive St.; Eames & Young, 1907; Tom P. Barnett, c. 1919

This was for a time the nation's tallest reinforced-concrete structure, and its two floors of indoor shops made it a precursor of the multilevel mall. The building and its elegant shopping arcade have been closed in recent years while their well-wishers hope for a viable renovation plan.

D31. LGL Center

1017 Olive St.; Mauran, Russell & Crowell, 1913; Ross & Baruzzini, remodeling

For one ample story above street level, a stone front with Roman-arched doors; then seven floors of gray-brown brick, the windows trimmed in cream-colored terra-cotta; at the top, a two-story colonnade of the same creamy terra-cotta. This harmonious composition was home to the Laclede Gas Light Co. and has lately been remodeled as the LGL Center.

D32. Merchandise Mart

1000 Washington Ave.; Isaac S. Taylor, 1888

Great chunks of red granite, polished and rusticated; virtuosic displays of bricklaying above, culminating in a red brick colonnade; red terra-cotta trims; and surmounting all a rich copper cornice. This fine old commercial building is the essence of St. Louis solidity. Rehabbing was interrupted in 1987 by a shortage of money, caused by an oversupply of Downtown office space, old and new.

D33. Hadley Square

1101 Lucas Ave.; Isaac S. Taylor, 1903

Rehab of the former home of the Hadley Dean Glass Co., a building whose powerful structure had to carry hundreds of tons of stored glass. The 1930 foyer decoration has Egyptian motifs etched in Vitrolite, a colored reflective glass once popular as a surface for walls and shop fronts.

D34. Lammert Building

911 Washington Ave.; Eames & Young, 1898; Mackey Associates, remodeling, 1985

A former furniture store, imaginatively turned into offices around an ample interior court. Tenants include the St. Louis chapter of the AIA.

D35. Washington Avenue

Early-20th-century St. Louis is better preserved along Washington Ave. than in any other Downtown section; the gaps left by demolition are relatively few, probably because many of the robust old buildings have continued to house garment-business tenants into the 1980s. Rehabbers began in the 1970s to convert some of the space to residences and artists' lofts.

48

D36. Mercantile Tower

Seventh St. at Washington Ave., northeast corner; Thompson, Ventulett & Stainback with Sverdrup & Parcel and Associates, 1976

Thirty-five stories, notched to give 16 corner offices on each floor. The plan is made an elongated octagon by stacks of three-story-high K-braces placed diagonally. This external steel structure stiffens the tower against wind loading, frees interior space, reduces total weight, and presents a dramatic street aspect. At 485 feet this was, until completion of One Bell Center (D23) a decade later, Missouri's tallest building.

D37. St. Louis Centre

Locust St. to Washington Ave. between Sixth and Seventh Sts.; RTKL Associates Inc., 1985

The answer to an old scheme for uniting Downtown's two big department stores with a covered mall. The interior, bright and airy, is better realized than the green-and-white outside, whose color, shape, and blank east wall clash with the prospect along Washington Ave. See color photograph, p. 23.

D38. Edison Brothers Stores building

501 North Broadway; Hellmuth, Obata & Kassabaum, 1985

Rich reds in brick, stone, and coated aluminum clothe this corporate headquarters building. Postmodern taste has given the street front Roman arch shapes and cylindrical columns, while the tower is capped with steep-pitched gables topped with barrel vaults.

49

D39. 555 Washington Avenue

Northeast corner of Sixth St. and Washington Ave.; remodeling and restoration by Kimble A. Cohn & Associates, 1987

The street front presents a meticulous restoration of late-19th-century facades, with entrance through a recessed and richly decorated half-dome facing Washington Ave. Inside, at the end of a hall, Beaux Arts decor yields to modern office space surrounding an atrium of unusual shape. Starting from a narrow clearing on the ground floor, it grows as it rises through five levels and is surmounted at the top by a 6,000-square-foot skylight. Old structural columns and beams are left in place in the atrium to support the skylight and a network of footbridges. The raw material of this enterprise was a group of 19th-century buildings united by a developer in 1898 behind a new facade. After a few years' service as a department store, the space was again subdivided and became a warren of cheap stores, garment workshops, and storage rooms, all abandoned by the time Cohn formed his redevelopment plan.

D40. Greyhound Bus Terminal

801 North Broadway; Schwarz & Van Hoefen, 1964

The dominant design element is a splendid cantilevered roof that spans the entire ticket lobby—waiting room and, as seen from outside, expresses the building's function as a gate to the city.

50

D41. Missouri Athletic Club

405 Washington Ave.; William B. Ittner and George F. A. Brueggeman, 1914

Exceptional craftsmanship and design come together in this palazzo, in which stone trim and balconies and patterned brickwork are surmounted by a heroic bracketed cornice.

D42. Security Building

319 North Fourth St.; Peabody, Stearns & Furber, 1891

Exterior stone trim is used through the third floor; pairs of windows between brick piers are varied with arched headings on seventh and tenth floors; and there are round attic windows. Lobby rotunda with domed ceiling was once home of the Third National Bank.

D43. Merchants Laclede Building

408 Olive St.; Stephen D. Hatch, with L. Cass Miller associated, 1889

Brick above stone, with a full-height stack of oriel windows, and inside some old-fashioned amenities like office fireplaces. One of a number of stately buildings raised for the banking and brokerage firms that concentrated in this vicinity after most commercial activity had moved farther west.

51

D44. City Hall

Market St. at Tucker Blvd.; Eckel & Mann, Harvey Ellis, 1896

Harvey Ellis was a designer and delineator of high gifts who worked for several eminent architects of his time; this exercise in French Renaissance style won a national competition for the design of a new St. Louis city hall. Other photographs show the original towers that were removed in 1936, to the detriment of Ellis's grand conception; the Hôtel de Ville or city hall of Paris, a probable inspiration to Ellis in his design for St. Louis, as it appeared after remodeling in 1873; the four-story interior court, completed in 1904 to the design of Weber & Groves; and the statue out front of Pierre Laclede Liguest. The sculpture is by George Julian Zolnay, 1914.

D45. Municipal Courts

1320 Market St.; Isaac S. Taylor, 1911

An august Beaux Arts composition in which differing window rhythms and a row of engaged columns are used to define a base, midsection, and attic story.

D46. Kiel Auditorium

1400 Market St.; LaBeaume & Klein, 1934

Massive streamlined classicism of a kind popular in 1930s government architecture. Kiel has an exposition hall on the ground floor and, above it, back to back, a 3,600-seat Opera House and a Convention Hall seating 11,500.

D47. Federal Office Building

1520 Market St.; Murphy & Mackey, William B. Ittner, 1962; foyer sculpture by Robert Cronbach

The upper stories of inset windows framed in brick and limestone overhang deep ground-floor walkways. A bronze lobby fountain symbolizes St. Louis's prominence in life on the river.

D48. Post Office

Market St. between Seventeenth and Eighteenth Sts.; Klipstein & Rathmann, 1937

Rigorously geometrical classicism in the manner of the Soldiers' Memorial (see D52). The outward sternness relaxes in a decorated Art Deco lobby with murals.

D49. Edison Brothers Distribution Center

400 South Fourteenth St.; a brick-clad reinforced-concrete warehouse of 1927, covered with architectural murals by Richard Haas, 1984

Choosing his theme from the Beaux Arts architecture of St. Louis's 1904 World's Fair, Haas decorated a homely warehouse with pediments, portals, windows, obelisks, and assorted masonry detail, none of it thicker than a coat of paint. King Louis IX on his horse is there in carefully executed perspective, appearing to guard the building's south wall. See color photograph, p. 21.

D50. Union Station

Market St. between Eighteenth and Twentieth Sts.; Theodore C. Link, 1894; train shed design by George H. Pegram

The asymmetrical grouping of varied masses, on a site with a pronounced downward slope to the west, makes this seem a much deeper and more complex building than it is. Its actual plan is a very long and shallow rectangle. Because of artful setbacks, the illusion of depth is maintained even as the observer draws close. The dominant style is

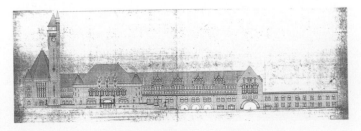

54

Richardsonian Romanesque, with touches of French Renaissance and a very striking clock tower whose engaged mini-tower (a working ventilation shaft) culminates higher than its parent. The occurrence of this device in other designs by Harvey Ellis (see NS18) has caused some to suspect that he participated covertly in the Link design. The double-barrel tower theme probably originated in the fanciful Neuschwanstein castle created for King Ludwig II of Bavaria in the 1860s.

Behind its Romantic front Union Station was a thoroughly modern, efficient, convenient, hygienic terminal that could handle 260 trains a day on 41 back-in tracks, all regulated by a pioneering electrical switching interlock system that prevented collisions.

After seven years of disuse Union Station reopened in 1985 as a shopping and convention center, with luxurious hotel rooms outfitted both in the old Terminal Hotel and in new construction under the train shed. Architectural work on and within the train shed was ably carried out by Hellmuth, Obata & Kassabaum.

On Eighteenth St. in the southeast part of the former station yard is the Power House (Mackey Associates, 1988). It's a new office building on the foundation of the station's old power plant; the chimney is original.

See also color photographs, pp. 9–11.

55

D51. Milles Fountain

In Aloe Plaza, Eighteenth to Twentieth between Market and Chestnut Sts.; Carl Milles, sculptor, 1939

The Mississippi, a young man riding a catfish, holds out a flower (perennially lost to vandalism) to the demure maiden representing the Missouri. A dozen other bronze figures cavort happily in the water. The genial Milles wanted to call his group *The Wedding of the Rivers*. Allegations that this name profaned a sacrament caused it to be changed to *The Meeting of the Waters*, but Milles and St. Louis friends defeated an attempt to veil the nudity of some of the figures. See also color photograph, p. 17.

D52. Two war memorials

Market to Pine between Thirteenth and Fourteenth Sts.; Soldiers' Memorial by Mauran, Russell & Crowell with Preston J. Bradshaw, 1938; Court of Honor by Eugene J. Mackey, Jr., 1948

The monument in temple form commemorates World War I dead. Its severely rectilinear classicism approaches the style of Marcello Piacentini in Italian monumental architecture of the same period. The World War II memorial, in foreground, is more somber and reticent, with a stele set in a sunken rectangular court.

D53. St. Louis Public Library, main building

Olive St. between Thirteenth and Fourteenth Sts.; Cass Gilbert, 1912

Outstanding example of a public building in the academic tradition of Paris's Ecole des Beaux Arts. The library is simple, symmetrical, clear in plan, well gauged in its proportions. The Italian Renaissance style is carried into a richly crafted and detailed foyer and main reading room.

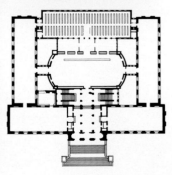

D54. Christ Church Cathedral

Thirteenth St. at Locust St.; nave and transept, Leopold Eidlitz with John Beattie, resident architect, 1867; Bofinger Memorial Chapel, J. B. Legg, 1895; altar and reredos, Kivas K. Tully, architect, and Harry Hems, sculptor, 1911; tower and narthex, Kivas K. Tully and W. A. Caldwell, 1912

Tawny sandstone is used in the 19th-century nave, white limestone in the newer porch and tower; inside, wooden beams support a ceiling that follows the steep-pitched roofline. Harry Hems's reredos, carved in England of Caen stone, rewards long and close inspection. A 1969 renovation and remodeling by Burks & Landberg aimed at outfitting the hall for the various performing arts. In the course of this work the old front organ cases and choir stalls were removed and a gallery was built across the back of the nave to receive a new organ and the choir.

D55. Shell Building

1221 Locust St.; Jamieson & Spearl, 1926

The gracefully rounded facade makes a distinctive presence on Locust St. where it meets Thirteenth St. It has been successfully renovated by Burks & Associates.

D56. 1509 Washington Ave.

Northwest corner of Fifteenth St. and Washington Ave.; Theodore C. Link, 1910

A shapely composition in which the piers become slender columns, flaring into Egyptian lotus capitals to support an ornamented cornice. The letter as well as the spirit of the Wainwright Building are honored here. Built as headquarters for the Roberts, Johnson & Rand Shoe Co., the building long housed the International Shoe Co. offices.

D57. Campbell House

1508 Locust St.; William Fulton (?), 1851

Last survivor of a double row of homes on Lucas Place, an early St. Louis private street. Robert Campbell, a prosperous businessman who with William Sublette was a partner in the Rocky Mountain Fur Co., bought the house in 1854. The building and most of its 19th-century contents remained intact because two of Campbell's sons lived on there as recluses well into the present century; since 1941 the Campbell House Foundation has maintained the property as a museum. See also color photograph, p. 3.

59

2 Midtown

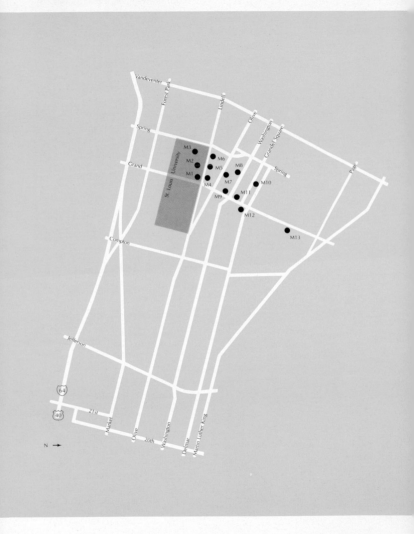

Through the 1950s Grand Blvd. was a destination for great numbers of St. Louisans and visitors. Its theaters, hotels, clubs, and restaurants challenged the best that could be found in Downtown, two and a half miles to the east. The brightly lighted strip ran from St. Louis University north along a ridge through a densely built-up four-block entertainment district. Then came Vandeventer Place, with its 19th-century mansions; the Odeon, where until 1934 the St. Louis Symphony played its concerts; St. Alphonsus Liguori, the "Rock" Church, with novenas so popular that extra streetcars ran on the big days; and Sportsman's Park, then at Grand and Dodier, a few blocks south of Fairground Park.

Urban decay and dislocations of the 1960s had a particularly destructive effect on Midtown, isolating it from the new expressway arteries that led from Downtown to the suburbs and taking away the old attractions one by one. Money and leadership for urban revival were concentrated in Downtown, with very little left over to sustain the flickering life along Grand Blvd.

The St. Louis Symphony cast a lonely vote for Midtown by buying a closed-down movie palace and converting it into an orchestra hall. Since Powell Symphony Hall opened in 1968, there have been several other signs of renewed life in the district, notably restoration of the Fox Theater and Sheldon Memorial, and some well-planned new construction at St. Louis University; yet a great deal remains to be done.

M1. St. Francis Xavier Church (St. Louis University)

Grand and Lindell Blvds.; Thomas Waryng Walsh and Henry Switzer, 1898; tower added 1915

Church in the English Gothic manner was built under Switzer's direction after the death of Walsh. Beyond it, facing Grand, is Du-Bourg Hall (1888), designed by Walsh as the first building of the school's new Midtown campus. St. Louis University, founded in 1818, spent the first 70 years of its life in Downtown in the vicinity of Ninth St. and Lucas Ave.

M2. Pius XII Library (St. Louis University)

On campus, southwest corner of Grand and Lindell Blvds.; Leo A. Daly, 1958; extensive remodeling and addition by Hastings & Chivetta with Murphy, Downey, Wofford & Richman, 1986

A severely crowded library on regular rectangular plan (at left in photo) gained interest, attractiveness, and comfort as well as room when it was linked by new construction (the Anheuser-Busch Wing, center) to an older academic building. Glass-walled stair and rotunda entrance of the revamped library have become the focal point of a new campus quadrangle, created by closing off a street that formerly ran east to west between the university buildings.

M3. Samuel Cupples House (St. Louis University)

On the university campus, southwest corner of Lindell and Grand Blvds.; Thomas B. Annan, 1890

Forty-nine-room granite mansion in the Richardsonian Romanesque style was built to face West Pine Blvd., in a block now vacated to create a suitable campus quadrangle for the university. The house with its 40 fireplaces and rich woodwork has been well preserved and serves the university as an art center.

M4. Scottish Rite Cathedral

3633 Lindell Blvd.; William B. Ittner, 1924

A 3,000-seat auditorium inside is occasionally opened to the public for entertainments. The front is a well-composed example of the monumental classicism often favored by Masonic organizations.

M5. O'Donnell Building

3663 Lindell Blvd.; Freedlander & Dillon, Lawrence Ewald, 1899

Built for the St. Louis Club and occupied for many years by the F. W. Woolworth Co., this French Renaissance mansion has become an office building favored by lawyers.

M6. Masonic Temple

3681 Lindell Blvd.; Thomas C. Young, Albert B. Groves, 1926

A grand pile of classical orders dressed in Bedford limestone, with gray granite trim and big copper medallions; it covers a site of more than an acre and hovers like a lofty acropolis over the cityscape as seen for miles to the south and west.

M7. Continental Building

3615 Olive St.; William B. Ittner, 1928

Skyscraper Gothic of good proportion, with hundreds of terra-cotta ribs making the building seem to soar higher than its 22 stories; abundant Art Deco detail animates the ceramic surface. Continental has been vacant for many years.

64

M8. Sheldon Memorial

3648 Washington Blvd.; Louis C. Spiering, 1912

Meetinghouse of the Ethical Society until 1964, and used by the society from 1930–1973 for chamber music concerts; acoustics in the 550-seat hall are regarded by connoisseurs as the best in the area for small ensembles. After working as a church for 12 years, Sheldon was taken over by a concert promoter in 1985 and put to use for performances of various kinds.

M9. Fox Theater

525 North Grand Blvd.; C. Howard Crane, 1929

Opened on the eve of the Depression as a king-size (5,042 seats) movie and vaudeville house with its own symphony orchestra, barbershop for ushers, and second organ to serenade people lined up in the foyer. After seeing only fitful use in the 1970s, the Fox was fully restored and reopened in 1982 as a performance hall for main-line touring attractions. The fantastic "Siamese-Byzantine" decor may owe as much to Eve Leo Fox, wife of the theater chain's owner, as to architect Crane; but Crane's skill as a designer of architectural space is evident in the ingenious lobby and stair layout. It moves large numbers of theatergoers smoothly through an entertaining labyrinth that affords them unexpected views of the foyer, the auditorium, and themselves. The climb to the upper balcony is 95 steps, but Crane makes the experience a pleasant one. Building tours are offered for people who don't want to wait for a show.

The St. Louis Fox has a twin in downtown Detroit, opened a month earlier. After long dereliction it was being restored in 1988 in preparation for reopening.

See color photograph, p. 16.

65

M10. Isaac H. Lionberger House

*3630 Grandel Square;
H. H. Richardson, 1886*

Completed in the year of Richardson's death by his successors, Shepley, Rutan & Coolidge, who established a St. Louis office. The exterior has been little changed, but the house sits denuded of its old residential environment. It has been occupied in recent years by Local 74 of the hotel and restaurant workers' union.

M11. University Plaza

601 North Grand Blvd.; Eames & Young, 1918

Built for the University Club, whose members and guests enjoyed the view from the top floor and penthouse dining rooms until the club moved west in 1975. Lower floors were rented out for offices. Lately the offices, mostly vacant for years, have been converted to apartments.

M12. Powell Symphony Hall

Southeast corner Grand and Delmar Blvds.; C. W. & George L. Rapp, 1925; Wedemeyer Cernik Corrubia, remodeling, 1966–1968

Built as the St. Louis Theater in a style inspired by 17th-century France. The St. Louis Symphony, which had never owned a home of its own, bought the vacant movie palace for about $500,000 and spent $2 million more on remodeling; the orchestra's offices were inserted into upper levels of the theater stage house. The profusion of gilt, cream-colored plaster moldings, red plush, chandeliers, marble, and mirrors suits orchestra patrons, while the hall's acoustical response, at first uneven and over-reverberant, was improved by various adjustments, including rebuilding of the reflective shell in which the orchestra plays. See also color photograph, p. 16.

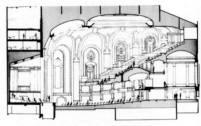

M13. St. Alphonsus Liguori Church

1118 North Grand Blvd.; Rev. Louis Dold, 1873

Familiarly known as "Rock Church" from the prominence of its limestone walls and 237-foot steeple, added 1893; baptistery added 1894. Side altars carved from Carrara marble, with onyx detailing. Windows, by Mayer & Co., Munich, were exhibited at the 1904 World's Fair. Mother of Perpetual Help Shrine, with annual novena.

3 West End

"West End" is an old name for a district of indefinite boundaries. It usually is taken to include the costly houses built along private streets on the north flank of Forest Park. East of the park, the West End spreads out for several blocks on each side of Lindell Blvd., about as far as Newstead Ave. A rule-of-thumb boundary on the north is Delmar Blvd. For the purposes of this guide we have taken Highway 40 as the southern limit, including the two square miles of Forest Park in the West End, along with the big hospital—medical school complex that extends east from the southeastern quarter of the park.

The West End's western boundary is not problematic. It is the city limit that civic leaders established permanently in a fateful home-rule decision of 1876. That perimeter, which seemed so ample at the time, has confined St. Louis at the same time that galloping suburban development carried the metropolitan area's real "west end" to Chesterfield, 18 miles beyond Kingshighway.

Most West End buildings date to the 50 years between 1880 and the onset of the Depression. Expensive materials, bricklaying of high refinement, and sophisticated Beaux Arts design went into West End homes. Their owners saw that churches of appropriate size and character were erected nearby.

The effects of post—World War II urban change were such that, by the early 1970s, three-story homes with ballrooms and carriage houses were selling for around $15,000. So far have attitudes changed since then that prices for the same houses are now well into six figures.

W1. McDonnell Medical Sciences Building

4565 McKinley Ave.; Murphy, Downey, Wofford & Richman, 1970

A teaching and research center for the Washington University School of Medicine. Utilities are attractively housed in the semicylindrical ribs running up the building's east and west elevations.

W2. Queeny Tower

Southwest corner of Barnes Hospital complex, Kingshighway at Barnes Plaza; Murphy & Mackey, 1965

Carefully studied and proportioned corner tower houses acute-care and self-care rooms and suites in a hotel-like atmosphere, with doctors' offices on lower floors.

W3. Park Place Residential Hotel

4399 Forest Park Blvd.; Mackey Associates, 1977

Large building but with domestic character and scale that fit its residential neighborhood. Interior courtyards are well suited for older residents.

W4. Engineers' Club

4359 Lindell Blvd.; Russell, Mullgardt, Schwarz & Van Hoefen, 1961

An interplay of forms developed from the equilateral triangle symbolizes engineering and architectural expression in the main structure, skylights, floor patterns, ceiling vault, and the 400-seat auditorium.

W5. Cathedral of St. Louis (the "New Cathedral" of the Roman Catholic Archdiocese)

4400 Lindell Blvd.; Barnett, Haynes & Barnett, 1907–1914

The structure, begun in 1907, is of steel and reinforced concrete throughout, with inner and outer concrete shells in the main cupola; the photograph on p. 72 shows the unfinished interior. The style, generally Romanesque outside with a Byzantine interior, was probably influenced by that of Westminster Roman Catholic Cathedral in London, completed in 1903.

The exterior cladding, below the green tile roofs, is gray granite. Inside the finishing materials include white and yellow marble in banded courses, scagliola (plaster imitating marble) to encase the steel structural columns, and a display of mosaic that at 83,000 square feet is reputed to

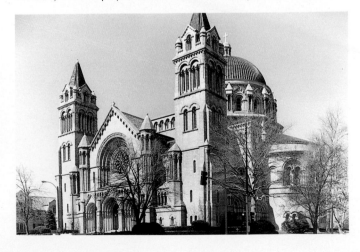

be the most extensive in the world.

All the mosaic has been well executed by its installers, Tiffany & Co., the Gorham Co., and Paul, Carl, and Arno Heuduck of the Ravenna Mosaic Co. The artistic quality of the work varies greatly, being most admirable in the chapels and ambulatories at the four corners of the building and in the narthex just inside the front entry doors. Blessed Sacrament Chapel in the northeast part of the cathedral, and its ambulatory with rich red vaulted ceiling, were designed by George D. Barnett. The chapel's iron gates are of massive and bizarre design, with florid decoration in the form of chains, rivets, punched holes, and other industrial shapes; they are reputed to have been part of the early Modernist decor at Austria's World's Fair pavilion in 1904. A somber vein of Viennese Secession style is evident in All Souls Chapel, south of Blessed Sacrament. Its squared columns and plain walls were decorated in 1929 by Rudolf Scheffler in white and black marbles, with dark blue and gold in the overhead mosaics. For it Barnett designed a gate incorporating motifs from the Blessed Sacrament gate left to the cathedral by Austria. Cardinal John Glennon, builder of the cathedral, is buried beneath the floor of All Souls. Recent remodeling of the organ display gallery above the main altar by Verner Burks.

See also color photograph, p. 13.

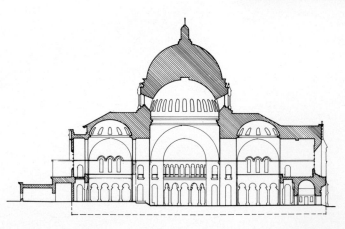

72

W6. Boatmen's Bank

4625 Lindell; Wedemeyer Cernik Corrubia, 1971

Well composed with main floor base, center section, and projecting top floor as cap. Stair tower provides vertical element.

W7. Park Plaza

Kingshighway at Maryland Ave.; Schopp & Baumann, 1929

The luxurious high-prestige hotel with lobby styling in Art Deco motifs rises to 27 stories in stages of roof-garden setbacks. Completed at the onset of the Great Depression, it remained a symbol of the good life through the hard years with transient and permanent residents. Recent renovations converted it entirely to apartment use.

W8. Maryland Place

North side of a block between Euclid Ave. and Kingshighway. A row of splendid old residences, now embedded in a commercial district.

W9. Lenox Place

A private street for early 20th-century yuppies who weren't yet in the mansion market. There are 27 houses, mostly built between 1903 and 1905 on smallish 50-foot-wide lots.

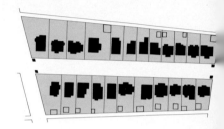

W10. Learning Center

4504 Westminster Place; Theodore C. Link, c. 1908

Across the street from Second Presbyterian, Link raised, for the Wednesday Club, a building with a low-pitched, deep-overhanging roof, strong horizontal accents, and an early-Modern air that was probably inspired by Frank Lloyd Wright's well-publicized Prairie House designs of the 1890s and early 1900s.

W11. Second Presbyterian Church

4501 Westminster Place; Shepley, Rutan & Coolidge, chapel, 1896; Theodore C. Link, church, 1900

Link followed the Richardsonian Romanesque lines laid down for the chapel by H. H. Richardson's successor firm. In 1931 LaBeaume & Klein designed the school wing that fills out this massive complex on the northwest and redecorated the chapel in a medievalizing style. The church nave has undergone several remodelings, the most recent of which (1987) involved successful repainting and relighting by Kurt Landberg.

W12. Lewis Place gate

Lewis Place at Taylor Ave.; Barnett, Haynes & Barnett, 1894

Triumphal arch of yellow brick and terra-cotta presides at the east end of a two-block street that becomes Fountain Ave. and leads to Fountain Park. Julius Pitzman's clients for the site plan had big houses in mind, but most of those built were pleasant bungalows.

75

W13. "Holy Corners"

A jocular name from the 1920s for the cluster of religious buildings along Kingshighway near the McPherson Ave. intersection. They are noted individually in the five entries that follow, with W14, W15, and W16 pictured from the left in the above photograph.

W14. Tuscan Temple

5015 Westminster Place; Albert B. Groves, 1908

The Doric portico faces Kingshighway, but the entrance is on Westminster Place. Home of Tuscan (Masonic) Lodge No. 360.

W15. St. John's Methodist Church

5000 Washington Blvd.; Theodore C. Link, 1902

Two main entrances, with Ionic porticoes.

W16. Angelic Temple of Deliverance (formerly Temple Israel)

5001 Washington Blvd.; Barnett, Haynes & Barnett, 1908

Eight Corinthian columns, with tall arched windows like those of St. John's Methodist.

W17. Baptist Church of the Good Shepherd (formerly Second Baptist)

500 North Kingshighway; Mauran, Russell & Garden, 1908

A grand Italianate ensemble in golden-brown brick whose color lightens by degrees toward the top. Auditorium and education building are joined by two loggias, with the campanile rising from the rear loggia.

76

W18. First Church of Christ, Scientist

475 North Kingshighway; Mauran, Russell & Garden, 1904

Careful detailing, interesting ornament, harmonious design in a building put up by one of the first Christian Science congregations in the world (founded 1904).

W19. Racquet Club

476 North Kingshighway; Mauran, Russell & Garden, 1907

Clubhouse where the Davis and Walker Cup awards were founded, and where $10,000 was voted to back Charles Lindbergh's flight to Paris. Big cornice, supported on brackets one story high, overhangs one of the city's grandest portals.

W20. Westmoreland and Portland Places

North of Lindell, between Kingshighway and Union Blvd.

Thirty-seven years after the first private street (Lucas Place) was established downtown and 18 years after the opening of elegant Vandeventer Place (demolished in 1947), these West End residential blocks were platted in 1888 by Julius Pitzman, the surveyor and planner who laid out most of the city's "places." Some early buyers moved out from both Lucas and Vandeventer to escape commercial encroachment. Eames & Young designed the east gate of Westmoreland, and Theodore C. Link did both the east and west gates of Portland. The gates are usually closed, and access to both streets is via Lake Ave. These, the most palatial of the private places, have been superbly maintained.

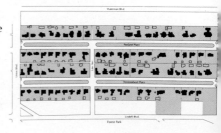

77

W21. No. 9 Portland Place

Shepley, Rutan & Coolidge with John L. Mauran, 1898

A symmetrical Palladian composition. First floor with its deep-raked horizontal stone joints gives the look of a massive podium. A plain wall at second-floor level surrounds rich carvings around the windows; over the attic windows, an ornamental frieze is surmounted by a deep cornice surmounted by a balustrade.

W22. No. 16 Westmoreland Place

James P. Jamieson, 1914

The Tudor look, painstakingly and munificently applied to the facade of a home built for Edward Mallinckrodt, Jr.

W23. Kingsbury Place, Washington Terrace, Waterman Place

South of Delmar, between Union Blvd. and Clara Ave.

The first two were laid out in 1892 and 1902, respectively, each with luxuriantly splendid entrance gates facing Union. Washington Terrace has the greater consistency of large lots and architectural scale. Waterman Place, formerly a public street, was converted to private management to assure continuity of neighborhood quality.

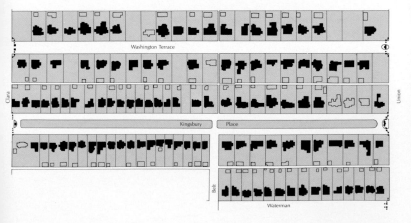

78

W24. Kingsbury Place Gate
Barnett, Haynes & Barnett, 1908

Rich as whipped cream but put together with control and unity. The sculpture by Clara Pfeifer Garrett is titled *Awakening of Spring*, modeled, it was whispered, by the daughter of a resident family.

W25. No. 11 Kingsbury Place
Barnett, Haynes & Barnett, 1903

Neoclassicism in a large-scaled, monumental, rather austere mood, with a cornice and balustrade at the top of two tall stories. Corinthian capitals on the engaged pilaster piers are the only florid touch.

W26. Washington Terrace gate
Harvey Ellis, for George R. Mann, 1894

A Romantic fantasy in brick, terra-cotta, and wrought iron. Gates like this advised visitors that they were entering very special, and private, residential property. See color photograph, p. 9.

W27. No. 37 Washington Terrace
Weber & Groves, 1902

The Georgian manner let St. Louis's native brick stand forth in some of the city's grandest mansions.

79

W28. Westminster Presbyterian Church

5300 Delmar Blvd. at Union Blvd.; Albert B. Groves, 1916

The generally English Gothic building of Bedford limestone in Scotch ashlar has its tower at the intersection of the L-shaped plan. Interior facings are of Caen stone. The woodwork, including pulpit, pews, doors, and choir loft, was designed by the architect.

W29. Union Ave. Christian Church

733 Union Blvd.; Albert B. Groves, 1908

Projecting bands of rusticated stone alternated with smooth courses animate the exterior surfaces of this building, its design adapted from Italian Romanesque prototypes. The well-proportioned tower and the auditorium's rose windows were endowed with commanding scale.

W30. Pilgrim Congregational Church

826 Union Blvd.; Mauran, Russell & Garden, 1907

Italian Romanesque in pink granite. Charles Eames did the church doors in 1933 when he was on the threshold of a distinguished career as a designer.

W31. Soldan High School

918 Union Blvd.; William B. Ittner, 1908

As the commissioner of schools and architectural consultant from 1897 to 1914, Ittner designed 50 schools in St. Louis and many more in some 25 other states, leaving an enduring Tudor and Georgian imprint on exterior design and setting the example of open, rational interiors. Soldan is one of his best. See color photograph, p. 14.

W32. Clark School

1020 Union Blvd.; William B. Ittner, 1907

Monumental composition in which classroom lighting, ventilation, traffic patterns, and overall function were seen to as thoughtfully as was the look of the building.

81

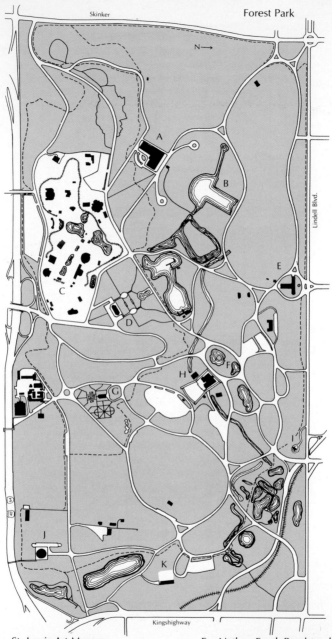

Forest Park

A. St. Louis Art Museum
B. Grand Basin
C. St. Louis Zoo
D. World's Fair Pavilion
E. Jefferson Memorial

F. Nathan Frank Bandstand
G. Jewel Box
H. Municipal Opera
I. Park Keeper's House
J. McDonnell Planetarium
K. Steinberg Skating Rink

82

W33. Forest Park

It amounted to about 1,375 acres when the city took it over in 1876, and by reckoning of the Parks & Recreation Department has lost only 80 acres since. The first plan for Forest Park development was published the same year, the work of Maximillian G. Kern, Andrew McKinley, Julius Pitzman, Henry Flad, and Theodore C. Link. Some of the drives in the east half of the park remain today as they were set out in the plan, and the original park keeper's house of 1876 still stands on the north side of the park near the Union Blvd. entrance. The western half owes most of its present appearance to work done by the Louisiana Purchase Exposition Co. in a decade of cleanup, relandscaping, and new construction following the 1904 World's Fair. Further changes in both ends of the park were brought about after World War I by the job of confining the unruly River des Peres in a new underground channel.

W34. Jefferson Memorial

Forest Park, DeBaliviere Ave. entrance; Isaac S. Taylor and Oscar Enders, 1913

Built for the Missouri Historical Society by the Louisiana Purchase Exposition Co. from proceeds of the 1904 World's Fair. Inside the central porch, lately weatherproofed with glass, is Karl Bitter's splendid statue of Thomas Jefferson, showing him restless and a little awkward as contemporaries described him. Another fine Bitter sculpture, a high-relief bronze on the east wall of the porch, depicts the signing of the Louisiana Purchase treaty by Robert Livingston, James Monroe, and Barbé Marbois.

83

W35. St. Louis Art Museum

Forest Park; Cass Gilbert, 1904

Limestone-clad Roman Revival building put up for the World's Fair, the only masonry structure among temporary exhibition palaces of wood and plaster. An auditorium was added on the south by Murphy & Mackey, 1959; it was enclosed in a new administrative wing by Howard Needles Tammen & Bergendorff, 1980. A sculpture court of the same year, by Zion & Breen, separates the south wing from the main museum at ground level. Interiors of the old east and west wings were most recently remodeled in 1975–1977 and 1985–1987, respectively, by Hardy Holzman Pfeiffer Associates and SMP/Smith-Entzeroth. A mezzanine floor was inserted in the west wing by Charles Nagel, 1961; recent changes in the west wing include a Postmodern staircase by Charles Moore.

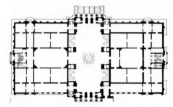

The equestrian statue of St. Louis in front of the museum is by Charles H. Niehaus. A plaster cast presided near the fair's main entrance off Lindell Blvd; the bronze cast was made after the fair for installation on the present site.

W36. Kiener Entrance, St. Louis Zoo

Forest Park, north Zoo entrance; Bernoudy, Mutrux & Bauer, 1966

The Zoo's best-defined entrance, at the foot of Art Hill, is a concave arcade of brick columns and round-arched openings. Serpentine walls of the same brick extend on either side.

84

W37. Zoo Bird Cage

Forest Park

Built by the Smithsonian Institution for the 1904 World's Fair, then purchased by the city for the zoo that was established in 1916. This walk-through aviary, 228 feet long, 84 feet wide, and 50 feet high, was the first of its kind and is thought to be still the largest in the world.

W38. World's Fair Pavilion

Forest Park; Henry Wright with George E. Kessler, landscape, c. 1909

In return for the use of Forest Park for the World's Fair, the Louisiana Purchase Exposition Co. promised the city of St. Louis to clean up and re-landscape the grounds. A budget surplus led the fair company to go further and construct two substantial new buildings: the Jefferson Memorial (W34) and a refreshment pavilion that occupies part of the site of the Fair's big Missouri Building.

W39. Municipal Opera

Forest Park; Arcade: Murphy & Wischmeyer, 1939

Open-air theater seating 12,000 with one of the largest outdoor stages in the world. The opera developed from the Pageant & Masque of St. Louis in 1914 and the Pageant of Independence in 1918 and was launched in 1919. Some seats are free. The neo-classic arcade encloses offices and service structures and gives the complex a pleasant and dignified public face.

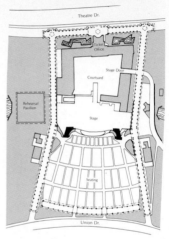

W40. Nathan Frank Bandstand

In Forest Park "Duck Pond" across from Municipal Opera entrance; Helfensteller, Hirsch & Watson, 1925

This Beaux Arts pavilion, accessible only by boat, serves rarely for concerts but constantly as charming ornament. It replaced a pagoda of Near East extraction built for the park's opening.

W41. Jewel Box

Forest Park; William C. E. Becker, engineer, 1936

Stepped-pyramid form was popular in tall buildings of the 1920s and 1930s; this monumental greenhouse makes good use of the Art Deco motif. Nearby is the gate, by Louis E. Mullgardt, of Vandeventer Place, an early private street of mansions that was destroyed to make way for Cochran Veterans Hospital.

W42. St. Louis Community College at Forest Park

Oakland Ave. between Macklind and Highlander Aves.; Harry Weese & Associates, 1969

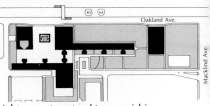

Continuous bands of deep-set windows, a notched shadow line, and top-floor slab with no fenestration might seem to extend to a vanishing point except for robust projections for utilities and stairways on the south side and openings on the north side. A sunken court at the west end provides transition between the linear campus and the public street and is an occasional gathering place. On site of the old Forest Park Highlands amusement park, which burned in 1963.

87

W43. St. Louis Arena

5700 Oakland Ave.; Gustel R. Kiewitt, 1929

Its roof is perhaps the largest extant example of "lamellar" construction. As Kiewitt used the word, lamellas were relatively short, light wooden members that two men could lift and bolt into place in a vaulted grid; the lozenge-shaped openings in the grid were small enough to be bridged by ordinary roof decking. The system fell out of use because construction was labor-consuming and the arched structure was less tolerant of uneven roof loading than conventional trusses. The Arena roof is oblong, with a 165-foot-wide section of vault meeting two half domes. It covers 17,500 spectators sitting around a hockey rink.

W44. McDonnell Planetarium

Forest Park; Hellmuth, Obata & Kassabaum, with Albert Alper, structural engineer, 1963

Now part of the St. Louis Science Center but still popularly known as the Planetarium. Thin-shell concrete cast in the shape of a hyperboloid, described by a straight line held at a constant angle while rotated around a vertical axis.

W45. Delmar-DeBaliviere Building

5654 Delmar Blvd.; Isadore Shank, 1928

Black and red terra-cotta panels with geometrical designs clothe the street front, which was for shops. Two stories of efficiency apartments above are clad in black brick, animated by corbels and decorative brickwork. Shank was clearly influenced by Frank Lloyd Wright's "textile block" buildings in California and Arizona.

88

W46. Bi-State Bus Facility

Southwest corner of DeBaliviere Ave. and Delmar Blvd.; Ripley Rasmus for Mackey Associates, 1986

The basic plan of this bus maintenance building was provided by a consultant and served for two other Bi-State facilities, both in industrial parks. The public is not allowed in any of the bus barns, but this one is in urban surroundings, so the architect tried to relieve its austerity and screen pedestrians from the parade of buses. He laid out a fenced courtyard-parking lot along DeBaliviere and gave the building front a formal center with a gently Postmodern clock tower containing elevators and stairs. Red and orange-beige bricks give color contrast, while turquoise-glazed bricks are distributed in small accent panels. Bands of glass block let in daylight and define building profile at night. Trims, ledges, and copings are of cast concrete.

W47. Smith House

5725 Lindell Blvd.; Gary Glenn, 1985

The clients were devoted to architectural and decorative Modernism; at the same time they wanted to present a formal street front in the spirit of Beaux Arts mansions farther east on Lindell. The result is an L-shaped house with more than 6,000 square feet enclosed on two floors, a mezzanine study bringing the east end of the street front to three floors, and a screen-like construction to extend the facade westward across the driveway. The finish material is white plaster, the structure wood with some steel reinforcement.

4 Near South Side

The Near South Side is the older South Side, with many buildings from the mid-19th century. It is further distinguished by its strongly German ethnic background, its two massive breweries, its neighborhoods of costly residences, and the expanse of Soulard Market. On its north and east sides this district is bounded by rails and industrial activities that date to the 1850s. The other two boundaries have to be defined arbitrarily; we have placed them along Grand Blvd. and Cherokee St.

Numerous blocks of quite varied house types reward random exploration, and there are four districts—three residential, one commercial—of particular interest for their maintenance of historic fabric and their continuing active life.

Soulard is the city's oldest neighborhood and the one with its post-colonial development the most nearly intact. Around its central farmers' market grew a community of German, Hungarian, Croatian, Italian, and Serbian immigrants who walked to work in breweries, factories, and heavy industries, lived in mutual-support groups, built big ethnic churches, and spoke their own languages. On what had been orchards and farms owned by French settlers with Spanish land grants were built houses and flats in blocks with corner stores. Some alley houses survive. A flat probably unique to St. Louis has second-floor units accessed via a tunnel-like corridor from the sidewalk through the house to back-porch stairways. Many distinctive buildings, in near-ruin two decades ago, have been regained as dwellings and for commercial uses.

In LaSalle Park sturdy old residences of good ensemble styles were pulled back from the brink and renovated in limited-access blocks. North parts of the area were cleared for new residential and commercial uses. All this received substantial support from Ralston Purina Co.

Lafayette Square, originally a restricted district of fine houses facing Lafayette Park and along adjacent streets, declined to a concentration of shabby boarding houses, then was regained largely by owner rehabilitation.

Cherokee Street east of Jefferson Ave. has the city's primary concentration of antiques dealers. Many of them moved from the high-rent Central West End to infuse this area with this specialized new use while keeping its old small-shop character.

91

NS1. Ralston Purina Co.

Checkerboard Square (Chouteau Ave. between Ninth and Tenth Sts.); Hellmuth, Obata & Kassabaum, 1969

World headquarters tower of sandblasted concrete rises from a three-story sloping base that encloses a full-length reception and exhibition floor. Mechanical services are directly above this space, with offices on the 12 floors that make up the straight-sided shaft.

NS2. St. Vincent de Paul Church

Ninth St. at Park Ave.; M. L. Clark, George I. Barnett, 1845; Franz Saler, vestibule and facade, c. 1849

The old relationship of this Italianate church to the Soulard area has been broken by the intervening slash of interstate highway. A good Pfeffer organ of 1874, built nearby on Marion St., is still at work in the gallery.

NS3. St. John Nepomuk Church

Eleventh St. at Lafayette Ave.; 1870, 1897; Wedemeyer Cernik Corrubia, preservation

Founded by immigrants of the late 1840s as the first Czech parish in the New World. A tornado destroyed all but the east front in 1896 and the church was quickly rebuilt to the original plan.

NS4. Soulard Market

Seventh to Ninth St., Carroll St. to Lafayette Ave.; Albert E. Osburg, 1929

The central building is modeled on Brunelleschi's Foundling Hospital in Florence; it is flanked by four sheds containing 275 stalls, all busy late in the week. The site was given to the public by Julie Soulard, widow of the surveyor of Upper Louisiana.

NS5. A block of Eighth Street

Trinity Lutheran Church is at right in this elevation drawing of a block near Soulard Market. View to west, between Geyer Ave. and Soulard St.

NS6. Sts. Peter and Paul Church

Eighth St. at Allen Ave.; Franz Georg Himpler, 1875

Church of a German parish founded in 1849. Its old constituency melted away after World War II, but the building was maintained in good condition and now enjoys the benefits of renewed life in its parish. Quoins and buttress facings were painted black in an odd decorative gesture of many years ago.

93

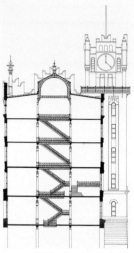

NS7. Anheuser-Busch Brew House and gates

Part of a 142-acre complex along Pestalozzi St. from First to Thirteenth Sts.; Widman & Walsh and C. D. Boisselier, 1892

The clock tower presides over a conglomeration of modern forms mingled with German Romanesque. Inside, iron chandeliers in the shape of hop vines are suspended in a five-story lightwell. The famous Clydesdales are housed in a round stable (E. Jungenfeld & Co., 1885) that is finished in polished stone, terracotta, paneling, and stained glass.

The illustrations show the Brew House (below, left), an east-to-west section through that building, and Warehouse No. 6 (below, right), which is decorated with vigorous and expressive details. See also color photograph, p. 8.

NS8. St. Agatha Church

Ninth and Utah Sts.; Joseph Stauder, 1885

The harmony as well as the variety of old St. Louis's brick architecture is evident in the neighborly coexistence of this Gothic-revival church with the brewery complex two blocks north.

94

NS9. Chatillon-DeMenil House

DeMenil Place (Thirteenth St.) at Cherokee St.; Henry Pitcher, 1863

Part of an older house, built around 1849, is incorporated in this mansion. It was put up by Henry Chatillon, hunter and guide of Francis Parkman's Oregon Trail expedition. Chatillon sold the property to Dr. Nicholas N. DeMenil, who made a fortune in real estate and in the city's first drugstore chain. DeMenil greatly enlarged the 1849 house and put an Ionic porch on it, preferring however to have the main entry on the back or Thirteenth St. side. His son, Alexander DeMenil, a lawyer and editor of literary journals, occupied the mansion until his death in 1928. The building of I-55 threatened it with demolition; it was saved by the efforts of Landmarks Association of St. Louis. Restoration and preservation work since 1964 by Gerhardt Kramer. Open. Visitors may phone for hours and street directions.

NS10. Lemp Brewery

Broadway, Cherokee St., and Lemp Ave.; E. Jungenfeld, 1885; Guy T. Norton, fermenting house, 1907

Begun in 1862 and once the city's biggest brewery. Since Prohibition shut off the beer in 1919, the complex has been owned by International Shoe Co. and, lately, by its parent company, Interco, which uses the brewery for warehouse space.

NS11. Harris Row

1100–1118 South Eighteenth St.; c. 1874

A row of ten nearly identical detached houses, unusual among St. Louis developments. William Torrey Harris, the eminent educator and scholar who was superintendent of the St. Louis school system from 1867 to 1880, lived in one of these houses.

NS12. Lafayette Square

Jefferson, I-44, alley east of 18th St., setbacks south of Chouteau Ave.; park laid out 1836

Thirty acres of old common fields became St. Louis's first public park. Choice residences began to rise around it in the 1850s. The area was badly damaged in the 1896 tornado and entered a long decline, lately reversed by the diligence of a new generation of owners.

96

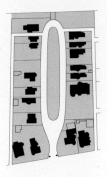

NS13. Benton Place

Off Park Ave. on the north side of Lafayette Park; opened in 1867

This was the second of St. Louis's private streets, platted by Julius Pitzman. Gates symbolically discouraged uninvited visitors, and property owners had to sign a covenant regulating the character of what would be built, as well as standards of maintenance.

NS14. No. 21 Benton Place

John H. Maurice, 1870

John Albury Bryan is pictured in front of the house he bought and restored in the 1950s. Bryan's work prepared the way for subsequent rehabilitation of the Lafayette Square area. A longtime member of the St. Louis AIA chapter's Historic Buildings Committee, Bryan was the author of *Missouri's Contribution to American Architecture* (1928) and of a 1962 booklet on Lafayette Square.

NS15. Seib House

2323 Lafayette Ave.; Otto J. Wilhelmi, 1900

Richardsonian Romanesque, St. Louis style, with smooth and rusticated brick, polished granite, and painted stone and concrete trims, all in a rich brick red. The house has been well maintained.

NS16. Lafayette Square houses

Two blocks of houses along Missouri Ave. facing the west side of Lafayette Park, between Lafayette Ave. and Albion Place.

97

NS17. St. Francis de Sales Church

2653 Ohio St. at Gravois Blvd.; Victor J. Klutho, 1909, after beginnings made by Engelbert Seibertz, 1895

Seibertz wanted a stone building modeled on St. Paul's Church in Berlin; after years of difficult fund-raising, the plans were modified by Klutho and the building was executed in brick. The 300-foot steeple is still the city's tallest, and St. Francis de Sales's authoritative, shapely Gothic-revival profile dominates the south St. Louis skyline. There is no clerestory, so the aisles are almost as lofty as the nave. See also color photograph, p. 12.

NS18. Compton Hill Water Tower

Reservoir Park; Harvey Ellis, for George R. Mann, 1899

A gracious Ellis fantasy of mixed pedigree. As at Union Station (see D50), an engaged mini-tower climbs past the main tower, topping out in this case at 179 feet. It maintained pressure for water from the nearby reservoir, built in 1871 and still in service. See color photograph, p. 5.

NS19. Compton Heights

Bounded by Grand and Hawthorne Blvds., Allen and Nebraska Aves.

Fields that had been part of the old St. Louis Commons were subdivided in 1884. Five years later Julius Pitzman laid out Longfellow and Hawthorne Blvds. The ample residences in this neighborhood, built in many styles from the 1890s on, have been well kept over the years.

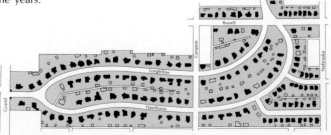

98

NS20. Charles Stockstrom House

3400 Russell Blvd.; Ernst C. Janssen, 1908

Grand and glorious on its far-spreading lot, like a Jacobean country manor set down in the city. The materials are tan brick, salmon terra-cotta, and copper under a roof of flat red tiles; the style is approximately German of the 17th century, and every part looks at peace with itself and its neighbors. It is still owned by the Stockstrom family.

NS21. Chapel, University Hospital at St. Louis University Medical Center

1325 South Grand Blvd.; Ralph Adams Cram, 1933

Late Gothic revival by a hardy American medievalist. Renovation by Burks Associates, altar sculpture by John Angel, stained-glass windows by Rodney Winfield.

NS22. Bi-State Maintenance Facility

West of Compton Ave. viaduct, south of Highway 40; Peckham Guyton Albers & Viets, 1983

Cheerful white and blue cladding and a lively composition help this bus barn enhance a bleak urban-renewal landscape.

99

5 South Side

St. Louisans generalize freely about South St. Louis. Its residents are Germans—"Dutch"—who like neat yards, flowers, quiet neighborhoods, beer, and a cuisine in which meat and potatoes figure prominently. To some extent the generalities are true. Mostly German and middle-class, South Siders built houses to last. South St. Louis has some exceptional attractions, such as the Climatron, and they are duly noted here, but most of the pleasure of an architectural tour comes from wandering through miles of well-made, well-preserved, comfortable brick residences.

A distinctive kind of St. Louis house is known locally as the bungalow. Unlike the classic bungalow, the South St. Louis version sits on a narrow lot, 30 or 33 feet wide, with its roof ridge perpendicular to the street line. The front door is on one side, projecting a few feet under a steep-pitched little roof of its own. On the other side of the facade is a massive fireplace chimney. Typically the front door is topped with a round arch, the living-room windows with a flattened arch. Rusticated stone is used liberally in corners, window trims, and copings. The walls are, of course, brick, usually on a stone foundation. The St. Louis bungalow flourished in the 1920s and 1930s. Great numbers of them can be seen in the square mile or so bounded by Hampton and Gravois Aves., Chippewa St., and Kingshighway.

Another peculiarly St. Louis meaning is assigned to the noun *flat*. Here it is an apartment in a two-story building of two or four residential units, each unit having its own front and back entrance at ground-floor level. The yard is shared but the basement is usually divided, with the second-story unit having an outdoor entrance to its half of the basement. For obvious reasons families with children prefer a flat to an apartment, which is the term for a unit opening onto a stair or corridor behind a common entry. To see unbroken vistas of flats, turn west off Grand Blvd. onto Dover Place or Wilmington Ave.

An impressive display of 1930s Moderne or "Art Deco" styling may be seen in the environs of Francis Park. Some particularly florid examples are neighbors to Frederick Dunn's surprising St. Mark's Episcopal Church (see S26).

101

S1. Shaw Place

Between Shaw Blvd. and DeTonty St.;
George I. Barnett, 1879–1880

A block of houses in dark red brick with white stone trim, built for Henry Shaw, who expected rental revenue from them to support his botanical garden.

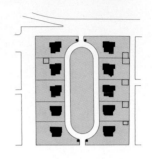

S2. Mullanphy School

4221 Shaw Ave.; William B. Ittner, 1915

Functionality, beauty, and monumentality are well integrated by an architect who left St. Louis many outstanding school buildings.

102

S3. Missouri Botanical (Shaw's) Garden

Henry Shaw (1800–1889), a native of Sheffield, England, came to St. Louis at age 19, made a fortune in hardware, and founded this public garden in 1859 after years of planning. Within his lifetime the botanical collection attained international renown. The Olmsted brothers did a master plan in 1904 for future development, and it was updated by John Noyes in 1917. In 1972 Environmental Planning and Design, Inc., of Pittsburgh was engaged to prepare a new plan. Under its guidelines have appeared new buildings and facilities including Ridgway Center and the largest Japanese garden in America. Surviving 19th-century buildings and vistas laid out by Shaw have been maintained.

A. Ridgway Center
B. Linnean House
C. Climatron
D. Tower Grove House
E. Japanese Garden
F. National Council of State Garden Clubs

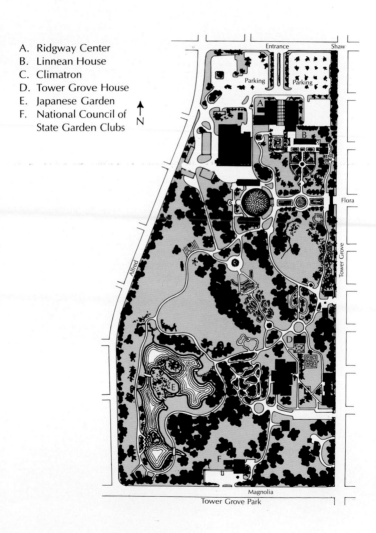

103

S4. Flora Place

The map illustrates the original relation of Flora Place to Shaw's Garden. Julius Pitzman laid out the private street in accordance with a wish expressed by Henry Shaw, the garden's founder, for a six-block residential parkway from Grand Ave. as a splendid approach to the garden's main gate. Both the garden gate and the street's west end are now closed, but the street retains its quality. The monumental Flora gateway on Grand Ave. is by Weber & Groves, 1898.

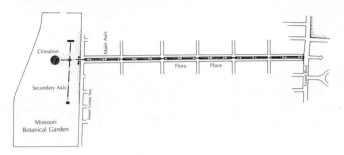

S5. Climatron

Missouri Botanical Garden; Murphy & Mackey, 1960; rebuilding under supervision of Environmental Planning and Design, Pittsburgh, begun in 1988

Spanning 175 feet and reaching a height of 70 feet, this is one of the most ambitious realizations of Buckminster Fuller's geodesic dome, and

the first to be weatherproofed with rigid Plexiglas panels. The panels leaked stubbornly around the edges, unwanted condensation dripped from the roof when it wasn't raining, and the climate-control system that gave the building its name never delivered the four distinct zones of temperature and humidity that were advertised from the beginning.

The structure is of tubular aluminum, with an inner dome, the one containing Plexiglas panels, reinforced by ties to an outer dome. In spring 1988 the inner dome was demolished and work began on construction of a new one, to be glazed with controlled-reflectivity glass instead of plastic. The $6.4 million estimated cost will include an entirely new climate-control system. Reopening for the Climatron is scheduled for late 1989.

The scant functionality of the expensive, leaky Climatron has been compensated by its great beauty. Despite the uncompromising Modernism of its exposed geodesic-dome structure, the Climatron has always seemed at home in the garden, enhancing and complementing its Victorian environment, the centerpiece of a favorite postcard view.

See also color photograph, p. 18.

S6. Henry Moore sculpture

Missouri Botanical Garden

Two-Piece Reclining Figure No. 2, 1960, was one of a pair of Moore bronzes given to the city for its new airport terminal (NC14). The two sculptures remained there from 1961 to 1969, when a loss of display space caused the donor to transfer the sculptures to the St. Louis Art Museum, where *Two-Piece Reclining Figure No. 1*, 1959, is installed. *Figure No. 2* is on loan to Shaw's Garden.

S7. Ridgway Center

Missouri Botanical Garden; Hellmuth, Obata & Kassabaum, 1981

A semicylindrical steel sunbonnet with plastic roof panels is carried on a pair of metal-clad boxes. The building was needed to channel visitors into the garden from the only ground available for a parking lot, in the low-lying north end of the Shaw property. It houses orientation talks, ticket booth, cafeteria, souvenir and plant sales, flower shows, auditorium events, and weddings—a useful addition to the garden's service facilities.

S8. Linnean House

Missouri Botanical Garden; George I. Barnett, 1882; Gerhardt Kramer, restoration

One of the few 19th-century greenhouses remaining anywhere, and the only one in the garden from Henry Shaw's time. Relatively small areas in glass. The main entrance makes notable use of ornamental brick patterns above a round-arched fanlight.

S9. Tower Grove House

Missouri Botanical Garden; Barnett & Peck, 1849

Henry Shaw lived here through his last 40 years. The three-bay wing east of the Italianate tower was added after Shaw's death, taking the place of a smaller servants' wing, and stucco was applied over the brick in 1919. Much original furniture remains. Open.

106

S10. Japanese Garden

Missouri Botanical Garden; Koichi Kawana and Karl D. Pettit III (Mackey Associates), 1977

A marshy tract was excavated to make a lake with four little islands. A bridge, teahouse, stone lanterns, dry gardens, boulders, waterfall, and a shoal of well-fed carp combine to make this 14-acre corner of Shaw's Garden a delight in all seasons.

S11. National Council of State Garden Clubs

4401 Magnolia Ave.; Frederick Dunn, Nolan Stinson, Jr., 1959

From the street one sees only a long, low wall of pinkish brick and mortar, banded with courses of stone, and a wonderfully sculptured grille of pink granite. Inside the building, brick and stone disappear, while glass walls bring in a panorama of Shaw's Garden. The property, on the south edge of the public garden, is used for Garden Club Council meetings and business and is not accessible to the public. The granite grille, carved on both sides to the design of William Talbot, was part of a fountain, shut down after attacks by vandals.

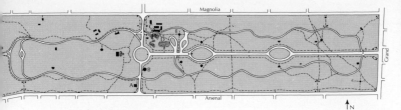

A. Arsenal St. Gate House
B. Dovecot Picnic Pavilion
C. Palm Houses
D. Romantic Ruins
E. Music Stand

S12. Tower Grove Park

The 285 acres of Tower Grove Park, stretched out in a narrow rectangle a mile and a half long, were deeded by Henry Shaw to the city of St. Louis in 1868, more than 20 years before his death. Shaw appointed the first board of commissioners that administered the park, and imported James Gurney from Kew Gardens, London's great botanical garden, as superintendent. Gurney, closely supervised by Shaw, carried out the spirit of an English walking park. Conservative management and devotion to Shaw's memory account for the fact that nearly all the park's 19th-century features remain today.

S13. Arsenal St. Gate House

Tower Grove Park; George I. Barnett, 1888; W. Philip Cotton, Jr., preservation

Rustic cottage topped off with a copper-roofed stone tower. Built for the gatekeeper, now contains park offices.

S14. Palm Houses

Tower Grove Park; George I. Barnett, 1877 and 1885

Built as steam-heated brick-and-glass greenhouses to keep potted palms and other ornamental plants through winter.

108

S15. Dovecot Picnic Pavilion

Tower Grove Park; Henry Thiele, 1871; W. Philip Cotton, Jr., presrevation

A pigeon shelter at base of the onion cupola was removed in 1891 for extension of the picturesque roof that seems to float above the picnic slab. See color photograph, p. 3.

S16. Romantic Ruins

Tower Grove Park; c. 1868

The burning of the first Lindell Hotel in downtown St. Louis, in 1867, yielded a large amount of ornamental stone. Several wagonloads were brought here and set up in semblance of a partly fallen facade beside a sailboat pond.

S17. Music Stand

Tower Grove Park; Eugene Greenleaf, 1872

Busts of Beethoven, Wagner, Mozart, Rossini, Gounod, and Verdi, Henry Shaw's favorite composers, surround this onion-domed octagonal pavilion.

S18. Hortus Court

Dutch colonial houses elegantly laid out in a court looking into Tower Grove Park.

S19. Holy Cross Lutheran Church

2650 Miami Ave.; Griese & Weile, 1869

The Gothic revival brick church with emphatic tower was built by a congregation that separated from Trinity Lutheran Church in Soulard and became the mother church of Concordia Seminary.

S20. Resurrection Catholic Church

3900 Meramec Ave.; Murphy & Mackey, 1954

A parabolic brick wall lighted softly by a ribbon of stained-glass windows near the roofline, with brilliant daylight descending on the altar through a round lantern near the apex of the parabola. Freestanding stone baptistery in front, slender bell tower at rear complete this suave Modern composition.

110

S21. Bellerive Blvd.

A street elevation of the south side of Bellerive, between Colorado Ave. and Louisiana Ave. Upper-middle-class single-family residences of the 1900s and 1910s that were solid, long-lasting, low-maintenance buildings with brick walls and tile roofs. The builders achieved variety and interest but stopped short of frivolity.

S22. Convent, Sisters of St. Joseph of Carondelet

6400 Minnesota Ave.; Aloysius Gillick, chapel, 1897; other buildings, 1841–1885

From an 1836 log cabin the convent grew into a unified cluster of brick and stone buildings. By 1885 a high wall enclosed all in a courtyard with a free-standing clock tower. Open galleries overlooking the court have fine wrought-iron railings and stairs on all three levels.

S23. South Broadway Shops

7127–7129 South Broadway; c. 1855

An attractive survival from a row of mid-19th-century shops near what was then the south edge of the city. Iron balconies of the second-floor living quarters shelter the shop fronts below. At rear of such family shops were often a kitchen and lounging room.

111

S24. Holly Hills Blvd.

Street elevation in 3800 block of Holly Hills Blvd., across from
Carondelet Park. Upper-middle-class homes of the 1920s and 1930s,
more fanciful in their decorative variations than the earlier examples
seen in our Bellerive Blvd. drawing.

S25. Bevo Mill

*4749 Gravois Ave.; Klipstein
& Rathmann, 1917*

Bevo was a nonalcoholic "near-
beer" introduced by Anheuser-
Busch before Prohibition, in the
hope of mollifying temperance
forces; the Bevo Mill began as a
family restaurant in which only the
lightest of alcoholic drinks were
served. Solidly built, magnificently
decorated inside, the Bevo remains a popular restaurant.

S26. St. Mark's Episcopal Church

*4712 Clifton Ave.; Frederick Dunn
& Charles Nagel, 1939*

One of the very few examples in
the world of Modernist design in a
religious building before World
War II. It is furthermore a handsome piece of work inside and
out, and the more remarkable for
having been achieved on a budget
of $75,000 for everything from
land to furnishings. Robert Har-
mon's stained-glass windows contain belligerent working-class
political messages.

112

S27. St. Ambrose Catholic Church

5130 Wilson Ave.; Corrubia & Henderson, 1926

Abundantly detailed Lombard Romanesque. This took the place of a 1903 wooden church built for Italian immigrants who had come to work in the clay pits and kilns at the foot of the hill, along the River des Peres. "The Hill" is still an Italian neighborhood, and St. Ambrose is its parish church.

S28. U-Haul Center of St. Louis

1641 South Kingshighway; Harris Armstrong, 1947

Built as the Magic Chef Building, company headquarters of the American Stove Co. Boldly modern for its time and place, the severity of line is tempered by Armstrong's fondness for surface texture and color.

113

6 North Side

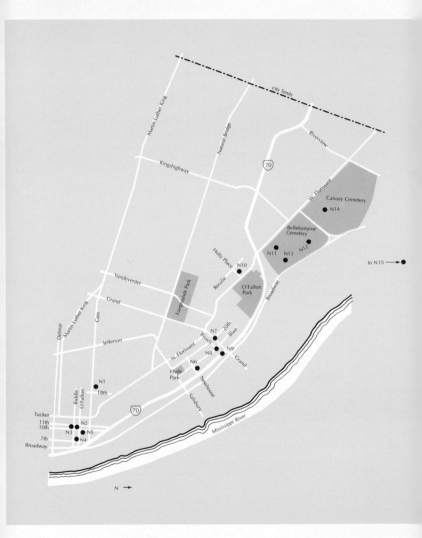

Germans in great numbers settled in North St. Louis, but their majority was not so large as it was south of Mill Creek and the River des Peres. They shared the North Side with Irish immigrants, Poles, and Russian Jews as well as native American whites and blacks.

Major green spaces and street names recall owners of extensive farm estates established after 1830. John O'Fallon's 50-room house overlooked his acres in what is now O'Fallon Park. The Edward Hempstead farm became a large part of Bellefontaine Cemetery. Bryan's Hill, in what became Fairground Park, was owned by Dr. John Gano Bryan (Bryan Hill School, John and Gano Sts.; Bryan St. was renamed Prairie Ave.).

The house of Capt. Lewis Bissell, c. 1828 (N9), probably the oldest structure in St. Louis, survives at 4426 Randall Place as a restaurant. From its porch Bissell could watch the river ferry that he ran at Bissell's Point, later the site of a water pumping station and now of a sewage plant.

College Ave. commemorates a long, narrow tract of farmland between present Warne and Linton Aves. that St. Louis University, then downtown, acquired in 1836 for a new campus. The area was still called College Hill long after the university decided against it and moved to Grand Blvd.

Between Downtown and affluent blocks around Hyde and O'Fallon parks, low-income dwellings ranged from alley slums to modest but well-kept flats and houses, some of character rivaling Southside counterparts—see the houses of Holly Place in entry N10.

Of the old ethnic divisions, the only one remaining is between white and black. The population of St. Louis within the city limits has come to be more than half black, and in North St. Louis the proportion is much higher, with several square miles in which hardly a white resident can be found. Many other North Side neighborhoods are integrated.

N1. James Clemens, Jr., House

1849 Cass Ave.; 1860

The double porch columns, window trims, and quoins are cast iron, a rarity in St. Louis residential building. James Clemens was a cousin of Mark Twain (Samuel Clemens), and the author is said to have stayed here on St. Louis visits. The large annexes on the east and south were built by the Sisters of St. Joseph of Carondelet, who bought the property in 1885. Now mostly unoccupied, it is owned by a religious organization that calls it Berean House.

N2. St. Joseph's Shrine

Biddle St. between Tenth and Eleventh Sts.; 1866; facade and towers added 1881

The original church rose in 1846 on Eleventh St. and grew swiftly after reports of an 1864 miracle attributed to St. Peter Claver. A century later the whole Jesuit compound—church, rectory, and school covering a block—was virtually derelict in the middle of a blighted neighborhood. St. Joseph's revival began in the late 1970s at the hands of a small group of friends led by architect Theodore J. Wofford. They had to persuade contributors, volunteers, and skeptical St. Louis Archdiocese authorities that the church should and could be saved. Their success in doing so, and the scrupulous nature of their restoration procedures, have helped reanimate the church's whole neighborhood (see N3). Wofford hopes in time to rebuild the cupolas on the bell towers. They were removed in 1954.

N3. Columbus Square

A thriving neighborhood of new middle-income housing has grown up around St. Joseph's Shrine (see N2). Good management of the nearby Cochran public-housing project has contributed to the optimism of residents about their near North Side community.

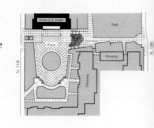

N4. Neighborhood Gardens

Seventh, Eighth, Biddle, and O'Fallon Sts.; Hoener, Baum & Froese, 1935

Three-story brick buildings wrap 252 residential units around rambling courtyards. Enlightened low-rent housing, created by private developers. The passage of a turbulent half-century has left Neighborhood Gardens a good measure of its genteel old garden-court serenity.

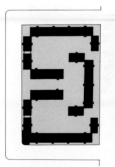

N5. Henry School

1230 North Tenth St.; William B. Ittner, 1906

Exceptionally fluent and expressive brickwork assists the skillful massing of basic elements in Ittner's composition.

117

N6. Newhouse St.

Street elevation drawing of houses between Eleventh St. and Blair Ave., Nos. 1113–1423 Newhouse St. Most are two-story or three-story apartments from around the turn of the century, remarkable for the variety their builders achieved with the medium of red St. Louis brick. Terracotta decorations, limestone, and glazed brick were used for accents, but the main fabric was red brick in many shapes. It was an expressive material in the hands of the master bricklayers at work in those years.

N7. Grand Ave. Water Tower
Grand Blvd. at Twentieth St.; George I. Barnett, 1871

First of three decorative towers that worked as standpipes, maintaining even pressure in mains from the city's first waterworks. The 154-foot column has a 116-foot brick shaft between an octagonal base of Chicago stone and the cast-iron Corinthian capital. It went out of service about 1912 but remained as a monumental punctuation in the middle of the street. See color photograph, p. 4.

N8. Bissell St. Water Tower
Blair and Bissell Sts.; William S. Eames, 1886

Tallest of the three St. Louis towers at 195 feet 9¾ inches, and eventful all the way up. There are balconies at the top of the granite base, 15 sets of triple windows along the spiral stair, and a circular platform near the top; one needs binoculars to appreciate the wealth of detail. See color photograph, p. 4.

N9. Lewis Bissell House
4426 Randall Place; c. 1828

An army captain from Connecticut put up his brick mansion (probably the oldest house in St. Louis), to overlook a river bend—Bissell's Point. The retaining wall that saved it from expressway demolition in 1957 was arranged by Landmarks, Inc., organized as a result of that danger. The house is now a restaurant and dinner theater.

118

N10. Holly Place

Street elevation drawing of the west side of Holly Place, from O'Fallon Park to the other end of the 4500 block. Upper-income homes verging on the luxurious, two and a half stories of virtuosic brickwork with granite porch columns, tile roofs, and decorative elements of terra-cotta or carved stone. The period is 1900–1920.

N11. Bellefontaine Cemetery

4947 West Florissant Blvd.; 1849

A large collective Protestant cemetery, established by civic leaders at the time of St. Louis's most prodigious growth, so that many older cemeteries in the path of development could be moved to a safe distance. Many of its first burials were victims of the 1849 cholera epidemic. A New York landscaper, Almerin Hotchkiss, was brought in to lay out roads and su-

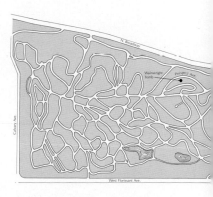

pervise plantings, which he did to good effect in a 46-year tenure. Catholics followed the Bellefontaine example by laying out Calvary Cemetery on the northwest (see N14). Jewish congregations established several cemeteries distant from the city, including New Mt. Sinai at 8430 Gravois Rd.

119

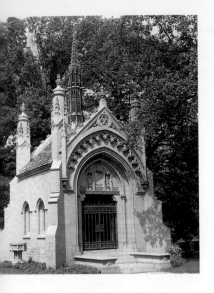

N12. Adolphus Busch Tomb

Bellefontaine Cemetery; Tom P. Barnett, 1915

For the founder of the brewing dynasty, a miniature Gothic chapel in smoothly dressed pink granite, bronze doors and spire, and stained glass. Crisply executed carvings adorn the pinnacles and the recesses above the doorway.

N13. Wainwright Tomb

Bellefontaine Cemetery; Louis Sullivan, 1892

One of three remaining Sullivan works in St. Louis, the tomb was commissioned by Ellis Wainwright for his young wife shortly after Sullivan and Dankmar Adler had completed the downtown Wainwright Building. Smooth, plain geometrical shapes are decorated with bands of rich stone carving. The deep-blue mosaic ground of the dome ceiling has a single gold star centered over the mosaic floor with its burial tablets. See also color photograph, p. 7.

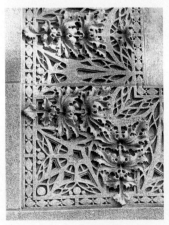

120

N14. Calvary Cemetery

5239 West Florissant Blvd.; 1857

The Roman Catholic counterpart to Bellefontaine Cemetery (N11), on 450 acres adjoining Bellefontaine on the northwest.

N15. Intake towers

In the Mississippi River near north city limit; William S. Eames, 1894, and Roth & Study, 1915

To get a look at these fantasies, go to Chain of Rocks Park off Riverview Blvd. a short way south of I-270. The older one, and the nearer to Missouri, is Romanesque with a conical turret. The second, in Roman revival style, has a stone balcony with iron railing, a quoined and fanlighted doorway worthy of a courthouse, and a penthouse with pedimental window headings. These curious buildings, perched on granite foundations that reach down around 100 feet to bedrock, housed intakes for the city waterworks on the west bank, as well as the workmen who had to keep the intake grates clear.

7 University City/Clayton

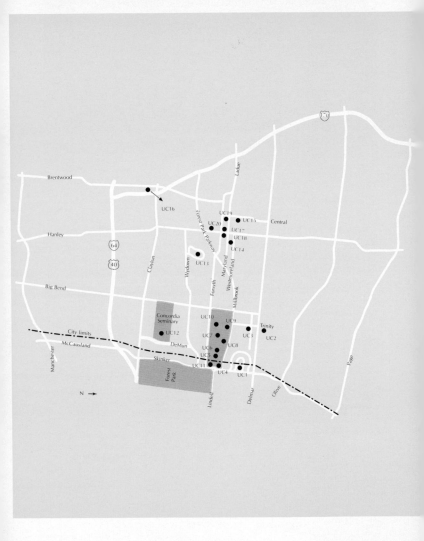

Around St. Louis, people speak of a place as being "in the city" or "in the county," a distinction reflecting the permanence of a political boundary drawn more than a century ago. Clayton and University City, however, particularly in their eastern reaches, seem to belong more to the city than to the great ring of suburbs around the city—a ring that now extends beyond the Missouri and Meramec rivers.

That is because well-established building patterns in the city's West End kept moving west. Large single-family residences on small lots, luxury apartment buildings, private streets, all crossed the city limit to spread deep into Clayton and University City.

University City began as a post—World's Fair planned development by Edward G. Lewis, a man in whose character the qualities of publishing genius, supersalesman, and visionary were well mixed, together with other tendencies that made him subject to repeated federal prosecution for fraud. Those prosecutions caused Lewis's St. Louis operation to wither before most of the construction could be realized. Surviving Lewis works are the rococo City Hall, a printing plant at the rear, the first unit of a People's University, and the pair of concrete lions on high podiums that flank Delmar Blvd.

Clayton is older than University City, but not by much. It was created to be the new St. Louis County seat in 1877, the year after St. Louis took the fateful step of adopting a home-rule charter, severing its ties with the county and fixing its city limits permanently.

City-county rivalry was old then and has remained alive into the waning years of the present century. In the mid-19th century St. Louis was a fast-growing metropolis in the far east end of a county that was otherwise quite thinly populated. City people resented the county court's power of taxation; they considered that their money was going to line the pockets of meddling, greedy politicians who represented rural interests.

The county seat had been St. Louis itself. Reestablished in open country west of St. Louis, the county seat remained a village in which county government was virtually the only activity, while St. Louis remained the seat of a new municipal county. Clayton did not even incorporate as a town until 1913, and until the 1960s its leaders would not let anything be built higher than the four-story courthouse.

UC1. Parkview

A private subdivision laid out by Julius Pitzman in 1905 on land made accessible by World's Fair development. The houses are smaller, more touched by 20th-century styles than the private-street mansions to the east. Photograph shows (from left) 6331 to 6311 Westminster.

UC2. University City Hall

6801 Delmar Blvd.; Herbert C. Chivers, 1903

Built by Edward G. Lewis as headquarters for a swift-growing national enterprise that included, at its peak, women's magazines, a women's newspaper, a bank, and a land-development company. Inside, a visitor can see the lavishly decorated spiral stair and, in a display case behind it, a scale model of the monumental civic center Lewis planned for University City.

124

UC3. Center of Contemporary Arts (formerly B'nai Amoona Synagogue)

524 Trinity Ave.; Erich Mendelsohn, 1950

In the last years of his life (1887–1953), the great German Expressionist architect saw a residence, a hospital, and five synagogues realized in the United States. For Congregation B'nai Amoona he designed a sanctuary with a steel-and-concrete roof that soared in a parabolic path from roots deep in the ground to a slender wingtip far behind the congregation, overhanging a glass wall. A large assembly room (right foreground in photograph) could merge with the sanctuary on high holy days.

A too-small lot of under an acre, and construction economies as the work proceeded, prevented fulfillment of all Mendelsohn's wishes. The roof was weatherproofed with tar rather than copper. To get more office and classroom space, the courtyard Mendelsohn had laid out north of the sanctuary was enclosed in the mid-1950s. Westward migration by members led B'nai Amoona to move by stages to a new complex at 324 South Mason Rd. (see WC13). The Mendelsohn synagogue was carefully remodeled in 1986 to enter a new life as a cultural center.

UC4. Washington University

Washington University, born in 1853, spent its first half-century on three blocks bounded by Washington Ave., Lucas Place, and Locust St. between Seventeenth and Nineteenth Sts. By the early 1890s it was clearly time to move west. The university directors began a meticulous procedure to find suitable ground, hire an eminent landscape designer to recommend the general plan of development, and choose an architect from among the best in the nation.

The landscaping firm was Olmsted, Olmsted & Eliot of Boston. In correspondence begun in 1895, it approved the site the directors had settled on just west of the city limits, a long east-west strip between Skinker and Big Bend Blvds., but strongly recommended the purchase of more land to bring the south edge of the campus to Forsyth Blvd. The extra 50 acres were duly acquired.

125

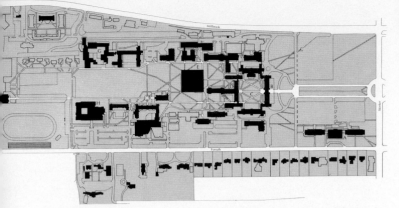

A. Steinberg Hall
B. Brookings Hall
C. Quadrangle
D. Ridgley Hall

E. Olin Library
F. Graham Chapel
G. Mudd Building/Eliot Hall
H. Simon Hall

In 1899 the school distributed the Olmsted drawings to entrants in an architectural competition. The winner, the Philadelphia firm founded by Walter Cope and John Stewardson, followed the general recommendation of the Olmsteds for a chain of quadrangles. Cope & Stewardson advanced a less symmetrical plan than their competitors and avoided the prevailing neoclassicism in favor of a modified English Gothic they had lately used at Princeton and Bryn Mawr.

The school delayed occupying its new buildings until 1905 to allow the World's Fair to use them as administrative offices. This deal repaid the university well, allowing it to put up ten of the projected Cope & Stewardson buildings in the first phase of construction, instead of the seven it could have afforded otherwise.

The orderly and attractive scheme of campus development set forth by Cope & Stewardson was continued by James P. Jamieson, who was employed by Cope & Stewardson in St. Louis. After the firm discontinued its St. Louis office in 1914, Jamieson formed a partnership with George Spearl in 1918 and continued to work on the Washington University project.

126

UC5. Brookings Hall

Washington University; Cope & Stewardson, 1901

Pink Missouri granite and limestone are the materials, late English Gothic the approximate style in the well-planned campus of which Brookings is the east front. The tower is penetrated by an arched passage leading to a spacious quadrangle. The map shows how this monumental entry is aligned with Lindell Blvd., main approach to the campus from downtown St. Louis.

UC6. Ridgley Hall

Washington University; Cope & Stewardson, 1902

Ridgley's manner is Roman Revival, but it goes comfortably with the late English Gothic of Brookings Hall on the opposite side of the quadrangle, and the materials are the same limestone and Missouri pink granite. The black-and-white photographs show a much-traveled passage into the quadrangle through the south end of Ridgley. The walk continues westward beyond Ridgley through an alley of pin oaks. See also color photograph, p. 13.

UC7. Graham Chapel

Washington University; Cope & Stewardson, James P. Jamieson, 1909

The prevailing campus Gothic, with pink granite and limestone. Inside, stone-lined walls into which are set oak roof beams, and an organ case of richly carved oak.

UC8. Olin Library

Washington University; Murphy & Mackey, 1962

Entrants in a national competition were instructed to make their library harmonize with nearby Gothic buildings on the campus, but not to imitate them. The winning design achieved that purpose with a strongly horizontal arrangement of granite, stone, concrete, and glass, the ground-level window wall being deeply recessed. Two of the library's five levels are below grade.

UC9. Mudd Building/Eliot Hall

Washington University; Schnebli, Anselevicius, Montgomery, with William W. Rupe and Robert Matter, associated; 1971

Campus-based firm won the 1966 international design competition for this law and social science complex. Adapted to steep slope with two stories on campus side, five on north, under folded and flat-plate roofs.

128

UC10. John E. Simon Hall

Washington University; Kallmann, McKinnell & Wood in association with Murphy, Downey, Wofford & Richman, 1986

First arrival on campus of the Postmodern, in a mild form, with round-arch entry, a streamlined cupola, and masonry imitating the colors and shapes seen in first-generation campus buildings. Deep overhangs shade ribbon windows, and there is a pleasant courtyard.

UC11. Steinberg Hall

Washington University; Fumihiko Maki, Russell, Mullgardt, Schwarz & Van Hoefen, 1960

Folded-plate roof and ceiling construction covering large spaces for gallery and auditorium on first floor, for library and classrooms above, and for sheltered plaza flanking the entrance.

129

UC12. Concordia Seminary

801 DeMun Ave.; Charles Z. Klauder, 1926

The quadrangle was laid out by Klauder, but lack of money caused the Martin Luther Tower to be capped at the roofline; it was raised to full 120-foot height to design of Froese, Maack & Becker, 1966. One of Klauder's handsome interiors, that of Pritzlaff Hall with its arched beam roof, is shown also.

UC13. Carrswold

Loop drive north off Wydown Blvd. between Big Bend Blvd. and Hanley Rd.

The private street of Carrswold has the distinction of having been laid out by Jens Jensen. The Danish-born Chicago landscape architect was engaged by Carrswold's developers in 1922 and delivered plans late in the same year. It was the only St. Louis commission for a man whose ideas about the harmony of nature and buildings drew warm praise from Frank Lloyd Wright.

Carrswold's 35 acres contain 23 residences, so individual lots are not large by luxury-home standards. About a fourth of the acreage, moreover, is common or "park" ground. Jensen got an effect of spaciousness by making his one street meander through a long loop, by concentrating his plantings close to lot boundaries and away from houses, and by using a long strip of common ground to screen the back sides of the middle row of houses.

The covenant to which property owners had to subscribe specified two-story houses with no garage doors turned to the street and forbade

130

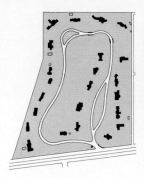

the introduction of any building "of the type called California Bunga-low." Houses began to go up in 1924, and all but four were completed by 1931. The latest, No. 18, went up in 1968–1969. The firm of Maritz & Young designed 15 of the houses; a sixteenth, done in 1937, was by Maritz, Young & Dusard. The photograph shows No. 4, the Keller House, by Maritz & Young in 1929–1930.

UC14. Hanley House

7600 Westmoreland Ave.; 1855; Gerhardt Kramer, restoration

The home of Martin Franklin Hanley, a founder of Clayton, was sold to the city for a museum. Decorative features have been scrupulously restored, and much of the furniture is from the family. Two-story porches front and back; original kitchen-laundry building. Black oak tree in front yard is re-puted to be the state's oldest.

UC15. Clayton condominiums

Nos. 120–134 North Central Ave.; Louis R. Saur & Associates, 1983

High relief in a complex street front, with brick and wood textures em-phasizing the impression of depth; roofs overhang, chimneys mount high, and the only neoclassical element in sight is the round-arched door. Courtyards open behind the facade.

131

UC16. Aerial view of Clayton

All these towers have risen since 1960, when architect-developer Bernard McMahon won a three-year campaign to overturn Clayton's old height restriction. McMahon's eight-story Clayton Inn addition broke the barrier. This view is northward from the University Club tower at 1034 South Brentwood Blvd.

UC17. Pierre Laclede Center

7701 Forsyth Blvd.; Smith-Entzeroth, 1965 and 1970

Two units, with 500,000 square feet of rental space and an equal amount for parking. The 17-story tower, closer to camera, came first.

UC18. Missouri Savings Association

10 North Hanley Rd.; Smith-Entzeroth, 1966

The roof of reinforced concrete, 127 feet square, was cast on the ground and raised to rest on four corner columns, 95 feet apart. The full-height glass curtain wall is set back from the columns, and interior space dividers are kept low so the broad ceiling plane remains unbroken.

132

UC19. Shanley Building

7800 Maryland Ave.; Harris Armstrong, 1935

A rare occurrence of the International Style in St. Louis. It was built for the practice of an orthodontist, Dr. Leo M. Shanley, and 53 years later remained in use for the same purpose by the original client's son. White stucco over concrete, with rounded corners. Armstrong experimented here with double glazing, letting the inside pane rest in a bed of calcium chloride so excess moisture could be dissipated in the building; the system was still in place in 1988 with only slight filming visible on the inner glass surfaces.

UC20. Interco Tower

101 South Hanley Rd.; SMP/Smith-Entzeroth, 1986

Ribbons of dark reflective glass turn rounded corners to make a full circuit of the building. They are separated by contrasting bands of aluminum curtain wall that set up a strongly horizontal stripe-like pattern. Wider metal bands cover service levels at the midsection and top of this 19-story tower.

133

8 West County

Since the late 19th century, big St. Louis money has headed west. Some mansions were built as far south as Lafayette Square and as far north as Cabanne Place, but they were left behind in favor of uninterrupted blue-ribbon development in what St. Louisans call the western corridor. That corridor now extends to the western limits of St. Louis County, 30 miles by air from the Arch.

In terms of architectural sightseeing this means that the sights are spread out over 50 or so square miles. Furthermore, many of the best buildings in the West County are residences that by their nature can be seen imperfectly from the street, if at all (see WC2).

Until around World War I it was usual for wealthy people to put up very large three-story houses on 100-foot-wide city lots. The money was displayed in rows of monuments, like the mansions on Portland Place or the mausoleums in Bellefontaine Cemetery.

The automobile let well-to-do people choose 10 or 20 acres of sub-urban woodland for a truly exclusive home site. Social changes led them to get by with fewer servants, or no servants at all. Twentieth-century taste discouraged ostentation; architectural designs became simpler in form, closer to nature. Pool, patio, and private park moved to the center of the good life.

By its demand for ever more roads and parking places, the automobile caused commercial buildings to be broadcast as far into the countryside as residences in a low-density, low-profile pattern. Only rarely did an ar-chitect produce something of merit in this market for glossy, quick con-struction. One who did was Frederick Dunn, by making the side of a warehouse an artful billboard seen by millions of motorists (see WC5). Another imaginative response is the "highway architecture" exemplified by Citicorp (WC14), whose high-tech buildings are designed to catch the eye of expressway motorists with a play of changing reflections.

WC1. Ethical Society

9001 Clayton Rd.; Harris Armstrong, 1964

The site tilts so steeply that heating elements are embedded in the entry and exit drives to melt snow, and passersby on Clayton Rd. can see little of the building but its roof. Accordingly Armstrong made the roof the dominant architectural feature outside and inside too, where a wooden ceiling follows laminated beams up to a skylighted peak centered over the meetinghouse auditorium.

WC2. Martin Green House

6 Upper Barnes Rd.; William A. Bernoudy, 1954, with 1964 addition

Bernoudy, a 1930s member of Frank Lloyd Wright's Taliesin Fellowship, has dotted St. Louis County with his engaging one-story variations on Prairie House style. Like most Bernoudy residences, this large example turns its glass walls inward to an artfully landscaped site, disclosing little to passersby. The photograph shows a small part of the private south face of the house.

WC3. Fred Evens House

9999 Litzsinger Rd.; Harris Armstrong, 1954

A commodious one-story house under a "butterfly" roof that looks like a shallow V in section and drains rainwater through central pipes. Exposed structural steel and glass walls likewise assert the Modern, while Armstrong's fondness for warm finish materials—stone, wood of various kinds, grasscloth—abundantly tempers the austerity of his straight-line structural composition, inside and out. All entry is from a large paved court at the rear of the house.

WC4. Morton D. May House

2222 South Warson Rd.; Samuel A. Marx, 1941

One of very few St. Louis residences in the International style, and the only one predating World War II. Marx, a successful Chicago architect specializing in hotels, and an art collector of importance, was an uncle by marriage of Morton D. May, then a young department-store executive and heir; May long afterward acknowledged that his own interest in art and in collecting was awakened by Marx. Most of the ground floor of the house, except for the kitchen wing, is given over to a T-shaped living-dining-entertaining room about 4,500 square feet in area.

WC5. Paul Flum Ideas Inc.

11100 LinPage Place; Frederick Dunn and Nolan Stinson, Jr., 1959

Built as a warehouse for the A. S. Aloe Co. and remarkable for the decorative use Dunn made of round ventilation louvers in the long side of the building that faces northwest, toward the intersection of Page and Lindbergh Blvds. The big ALOE name, seen in this old photograph, is gone now. The new owners have added a round office building at the north corner of the warehouse.

WC6. Monsanto's K Building

800 North Lindbergh Blvd.; Vincent G. Kling & Associates, 1967

There's nothing to see outside because K Building is below grade. Its showplace, accessible only by appointment, is this monumental hall used as an employee cafeteria, with ample room to seat 1,000. The piers and mighty ceiling beams of board-formed concrete, the unexpected changes of vista and level as one moves around, and the trickle of natural light from several shafts make this one of St. Louis's memorable spaces.

WC7. Temple Israel

Ladue and Spoede Rds.; Hellmuth, Obata & Kassabaum, 1962

The temple plan is two joined hexagons, with a folding wall that opens for seating of 2,200. School and synagogue are on opposite sides of a creek, connected by an enclosed bridge-lounge.

138

WC8. Parkway North High School

12860 Fee Fee Rd.; Hoffman/Saur & Associates, 1972

A variety of building forms and roof lines makes a lively skyline. The educational space is made flexible for changing needs by 30-foot spans on the first level, 60-foot spans above.

WC9. Community Federal Center

Manchester Rd. at I-270; Hellmuth, Obata & Kassabaum, 1977; Ladue Building and Engineering, space frame

The multifaceted structure of warm-toned precast concrete is a sophisticated composition of 30-by-30-foot boxes stacked in 10 levels, gradually reducing in area toward the top so as to leave 22 outdoor terraces. Over the lobby is a steel space frame with pyramidal skylights.

WC10. Jarville

Queeny Park; 1853, with extensive remodeling in the   30s

Red brick house with Greek Revival portico built for Hyacinthe Renard as the seat of a large estate. Remodeled by Jamieson & Spearl for Webster Tilton, and by William D. Crowell for Mr. and Mrs. Edgar Monsanto Queeny, owners from 1931 to 1964. St. Louis County purchased the estate in 1970 to create Queeny Park. Home of the National Dog Museum. Open.

WC11. Pappas House

865 Masonridge; Frank Lloyd Wright, designed 1954–1955, built 1960–1964

Theodore and Bette Pappas commissioned their house from Wright by correspondence and visits to Taliesin but were unable to start work until after Wright's death. The house is of the kind Wright called Usonian automatic, the first adjective meaning American, the other implying ease of construction with modular concrete blocks. Walls are a single course of blocks, made stronger with reinforcing bars and grout; the roof-ceiling slab is a reinforced-concrete grid with two-foot-square blocks carried in the interstices. Plans for an enlargement the Pappases wanted after work began were supplied by the Taliesin Fellowship.

Wright designed one other St. Louis building, also a residence. It is a late Prairie House type done in 1953 for Russell M. Kraus, on North Ballas Rd. Neither house is open to the public, and neither is visible from a public street.

See color photograph, p. 17.

WC12. Priory Chapel

500 South Mason Rd.; Hellmuth, Obata & Kassabaum with Pier Luigi Nervi, 1962

A triple tier of thin-shell concrete ruffles, of which the uppermost is a slender, 30-foot-tall belfry; rising above it, a 20-foot-tall metal cross. The festive look outside yields, as one enters, to the sobriety of a rotunda with central altar. It is softly illuminated by daylight passing through layers of Fiberglas polyester that fill the arch openings. Part of a Benedictine monastery and school. See also color photograph, p. 18.

140

WC13. B'nai Amoona

324 South Mason Rd.; Hellmuth, Obata & Kassabaum, 1986

Successor to the Erich Mendelsohn building left behind by the congregation in its westward path (see UC3). The hexagonal plan is better appreciated inside, where low, dim corridors diverge from the entry at a 60-degree angle and open suddenly onto a lofty sanctuary, lighted by a stack of six-sided clerestories.

WC14. Citicorp Mortgage Inc., St. Louis headquarters

North of Highway 40 between Mason and Woods Mill Rds.; Robert L. Boland Inc., 1981, 1983

"Highway architecture" means long, low suburban or exurban buildings that most people see only as they go by at high speed. These nonidentical aluminum-and-mirror-glass twins, one a parallelogram in plan and the other a trapezoid, are a supurb example. Their ends sharpened to 45 degrees, their sites abutting at the same angle, they intrigue the passing motorist with a play of unfolding geometry and moving reflections. See color photograph, p. 21.

WC15. First National Bank of St. Louis County

1350 Elbridge Payne Rd. (across Clarkson Rd. from Chesterfield Mall entrance); Ittner & Bowersox, 1986

Green-blue trim and reflective glass draw this building close to the lawn and trees of its site. Outdoor and indoor plantings are brought together by the sloping lean-to shelter on the bank's west wall. Its clear glass lets light fill the lobby, which is protected from late-afternoon glare by interior roller awnings.

WC16. Herman Stemme Office Park, Building No. 1

Roosevelt Parkway (northeast corner of Highway 40 and Olive Blvd.); Mackey Associates, 1987

A quadrant of terraced window walls is contained in an L-shaped three-story block in orange-brown brick. The brick walls rest on a limestone podium, and the windows of the top level are recessed within stone trim. Copper roofs the quarter-round of terraces as well as a 10-foot-wide bay with balconies that cross the east and north faces of the "L." Copper coping decks the rest of the brick wall. It's a neo-traditional or post-Postmodern look that is to be even more pronounced in the other six buildings planned for the Stemme complex. The look avoids both the jokey Classical "gesture" of Postmodern and the high-tech gloss of corporate expressway architecture. It aims instead for the reposeful, assured air of masonry construction, with depth in window and door treatment, and care taken to achieve harmonious proportions. See color photograph, p. 23.

WC17. Thornhill

Faust Park; c. 1810; Richard Bliss, restoration

The clapboard house of Frederick Bates, Missouri's second governor. Recent work has restored the upper part of a two-story front porch with pediment, and original 12-over-12 sash windows that had long been stored in an outbuilding. Open.

WC18. Citicorp Mortgage Service Center (formerly Fru-Con corporate headquarters)

Northeast corner of Clarkson and Clayton Rds.; Hellmuth, Obata & Kassabaum, 1982

Three three-story office modules with rounded corners are clad in alternating ribbons of white aluminum and green reflective glass. Blue-green tiles cover four taller service blocks and frame a quarter-round entrance foyer.

142

9 South County

Suburbs are ancient. Successful Roman businessmen bought property in the outskirts, either as an investment, to live at a distance from city noise and smells, or both. White Haven in south St. Louis County (see SC5) was purchased in 1820 by Frederick Dent, the future father-in-law of Ulysses S. Grant, because he enjoyed the tranquil beauty of the countryside; the Dents maintained a town house but spent most of their time on the rural estate.

A network of roads was already established. When the young Grant rode over from his military post to court Julia Dent, he followed a five-mile route that is still the shortest and best way to get from Jefferson Barracks to White Haven.

South County development was residential, bringing with it commercial services to satisfy the residents' needs. The hilly terrain, the bluffs along the Missouri side of the Mississippi below the mouth of the River des Peres, and the lack of navigable tributaries discouraged industry.

St. Louis's first railroad, the Pacific, introduced a new and significant phenomenon, the commuter suburb. To get from the River des Peres to the Meramec Valley, the rails had to climb a gentle path through the hills called Dry Ridge. It was near the route of an old Indian trail called, then and now, Big Bend Rd., headed for the "big bend" of the Meramec. The natural beauty of Dry Ridge attracted a number of St. Louis businessmen who, as soon as trains began to run over the first 15 miles of track in 1852, bought 10- and 20-acre plots along the right of way. They could live the year around in the clean country air, only 35 minutes by train from the downtown St. Louis terminal.

That was the beginning of Webster Groves and Kirkwood. Many fine 1850s houses—nearly all built of wood rather than St. Louis brick—survive in those towns.

At the same time, large acreages were being subdivided into lots for cottages built by ordinary wage-earners. They could afford the commuting fare and were as eager as the wealthy to get away from St. Louis's sulfurous atmosphere. Working-class people followed to take up the service trades. In this way there came to be established in south St. Louis County, before the Civil War, a pattern of social heterogeneity that is still evident in the older communities.

144

SC1. I-255 (Jefferson Barracks) Bridge

Mississippi River crossing at Jefferson Barracks; Alfred Benesch & Co., engineers, 1984

First example in the St. Louis region of a relatively new bridge type, and at time of building the longest tied-arch span on record at 909 feet. The longitudinal steel members carrying the bridge deck are in tension, like a bowstring, and are kept from downward deflection by cable hangers, whose fastenings at each end were carefully concealed by the designers in the interest of clean, uncluttered lines. The arches and their horizontal connecting struts are box beams of two-inch-thick Cor-ten steel. A second span began to rise in 1988 on the piers visible just south of the completed bridge.

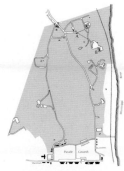

SC2. Jefferson Barracks Historical Park

In 1826 the U.S. government acquired 1,703 acres of high ground on the west bank of the Mississippi River south of St. Louis. It remained an active military base until 1946. The land is now shared by a veterans' hospital, a national cemetery, national guard units, and St. Louis County, which maintains the north part of the tract as a park.

A. Laborers' House
B. Powder Magazine Museum
C. National Association Civil Conservation Corps Museum (former Officers' Quarters)

SC3. Officers' Quarters, Jefferson Barracks

Facing Jefferson Barracks parade ground; c. 1900

Brick and frame building is occupied by an association of Civilian Conservation Corps alumni.

145

SC4. Laborers' House

In Jefferson Barracks Historical Park; Charles H. Pick, builder, 1851

This sturdy house was for civilian workmen employed at the U.S. Army's ordnance depot in the garrison's early days. Now part of a St. Louis County park and open as a museum.

SC5. White Haven

9060 White Haven Dr.; c. 1818; William Bodley Lane, restoration

Country house of Frederick Dent, a St. Louis merchant. U. S. Grant, stationed at Jefferson Barracks, met Dent's daughter Julia, courted her on weekend rides from the fort, and married her in 1848. As president, Grant, by then owner of the estate, made elaborate plans for retirement there, but mismanagement of his property caused him to lose White Haven. The house survived in good shape through ownership by three generations of a real-estate family, who subdivided the neighboring land but chose to live in the house on a nine-acre plot. It was purchased in 1986 by St. Louis County with assistance from the state of Missouri.

White Haven's date was long put at c. 1808, with its one-story kitchen annex thought to be earlier by virtue of its vertical-log construction. Documentary and archaeological investigations since the St. Louis County purchase have moved the date of the main house to 1818, while one of the logs in the kitchen has been dated by rings to 1838. Not open, pending studies of how to restore and exhibit the house without sacrifice of such features as original stair treads.

146

SC6. "Hardscrabble"

10501 Gravois Rd. on the grounds of Grant's Farm; 1854; Laurent Jean Torno, Jr., restoration

Ulysses S. Grant built this cabin for himself and his wife on the north end of his father-in-law's estate, in the difficult time after he resigned his army commission in 1854. The house stood in the northwest part of what is now St. Paul's Churchyard, a cemetery. It was moved to Log Cabin Lane, Webster Groves, by a real-estate promoter about 1900, was exhibited at the 1904 World's Fair, and was re-erected on its present site in 1907 by August A. Busch, Sr. Much restored, but back on property that was part of the 800-acre estate owned by Grant when he was president. Limited access by the public on tours of Grant's Farm.

SC7. Oakland

7802 Genesta St.; George I. Barnett, c. 1854; William Bodley Lane, restoration

Like Tower Grove, done for Henry Shaw a few years earlier by Barnett & Peck (see S9), an Italianate villa, this one done in white local limestone in even ashlar courses. Elaborate brackets support the cornice, and dentils decorate the deep pediments on the gable ends. Tower balconies, repaired and restored, rest on pairs of large brackets. The first owner was Louis Auguste Benoist, a banker; he planned his 485-acre estate as a gentleman's working farm, with landscaped gardens, four-acre lake, barns, smokehouse, and servants' houses. In the 1920s the western part of the estate, including Oakland, was bought by Lakewood Park Cemetery, which used the house as its administration building. Now owned by the Affton Historical Society, which has carried out extensive restoration and maintains the building as a community center.

SC8. Cardinal Glennon College

5200 Glennon Dr.; Henry Hess, 1931

A domed tower that may have been suggested by Bertram Goodhue's Nebraska state capitol of 1927.

SC9. Coral Court

7755 Watson Rd.; Adolph L. Struebig, 1941

St. Louis's most extensive monument to the Streamline Moderne or late Art Deco style. When the motel was built, Watson Rd. was U.S. Highway 66, main line to the Southwest and Los Angeles.

SC10. Loretto-Hilton Center

130 Edgar Rd., on the grounds of Webster University; Murphy & Mackey, 1966, with George C. Izenour, Robert Newman, Tyrone Guthrie, and Jo Mielziner, consultants

The 964-seat auditorium can be shrunk by closing off back and side bays, but the doors are rarely used. A thrust stage and shallow backstage have not kept this handsome, serviceable theater from playing a major part in the success of Opera Theatre of St. Louis, born here in 1976. It is also the home of the Repertory Theater of St. Louis.

148

SC11. Leif J. Sverdrup Business/Technology Complex

Webster University, along Big Bend Blvd. at Edgar Rd.; Sverdrup Corp., 1987

To fit a 70,000-square-foot campus building into an old residential neighborhood, architects made it ramble over a 550-foot length, tucked the second story under a deep overhang, and varied the roof profile at four points of articulation suggested by outside entrances.

SC12. Eden Seminary

475 East Lockwood Ave.; campus by Tom P. Barnett, 1914, with library by William Wenzler & Associates, 1968

Simplified academic Gothic in brick and stone, with a modern library building that defines and completes a satisfying enclosure of outdoor space.

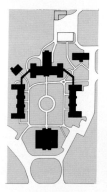

SC13. Hawken House

1155 South,Rock Hill Rd.; 1857;
William Bodley Lane, restoration

L-shaped brick house with its shapely two-story wooden front porch was moved in two pieces in 1970 from the 9400 block of Big Bend Blvd. when the church next door proposed to tear it down for a parking lot. The owner, Christopher Hawken, was the son of Jacob Hawken, an esteemed maker of rifles. A surviving invoice shows that Hawken was billed for 88,000 bricks at $5 per thousand. Maintained by the city of Webster Groves as a museum.

SC14. Sappington House

1015 South Sappington Rd.; 1808

One of the oldest brick buildings west of the Mississippi. The "barn center" with tearoom and giftshop is by William Bodley Lane, preservation architect for the house. Operated as a museum by the city of Crestwood.

SC15. Kirkwood Depot

Kirkwood Rd. at Missouri Pacific tracks; 1893

Demolition was proposed in 1941 in favor of a more modern and commodious building, but citizens of Kirkwood spoke out vigorously for their Richardsonian Romanesque station. It served commuters until the early 1960s and remains in use for Amtrak trains.

150

SC16. Kirkwood United Methodist Church

201 West Adams Ave.; Schmidt, Perlsee & Black, 1964

Light enters through a skylight in the ridge, through a Pentecost window that fills the west end wall, and through high-keyed colors in the side windows. Roof ribs and open 160-foot spire are of laminated wood.

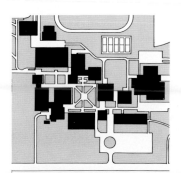

SC17. St. Louis Community College at Meramec

Big Bend Blvd. at Geyer Rd.; Smith-Entzeroth, 1966–1971

Buildings of red brick and light-colored precast concrete are arranged along a central walk that broadens into a quadrangle near the campus center.

SC18. Laumeier Sculpture Park

Rott Rd. at Geyer Rd. (southwest of Sunset Plaza), opened 1976

The former estate of Mr. and Mrs. Henry H. Laumeier, a stone house on 76 acres of rolling land, was bequeathed to St. Louis County for a park. The park became a receptacle for 40 large sculptures by St. Louisan Ernest Trova, one of which, *Profile Canto V* of 1974, is prominent in the foreground of the photograph. The Laumeier home, background, is the park's gallery. Besides freestanding sculpture, the park accommodates large commissioned environmental works, such as Mary Miss's *Pool Complex: Orchard Valley* and Beverly Pepper's *Cromlech Glen*. The park has grown to 96 acres and presents exhibitions year-round.

SC19. Alswel

Southwest end of Alswell Lane; Guy T. Norton, 1914

Built for William Lemp, brewery heir, overlooking the Meramec River valley. The intended effect was Swiss chalet, but neighbors called the main house (left in photograph) "Chinaman's Castle." In 1988 the remaining 43 acres of the Lemp estate, around the main house, had passed to a developer and were subdivided for the construction of luxury homes, the first of which rose on the site of the demolished guest house (right in this predevelopment photograph). Alswel itself was to be sold as the highest-priced home in the subdivision. Four other Alswel out-buildings, absorbed in an earlier subdivision, may be seen along Alswell Lane.

152

SC20. General American National Service Center

13045 Tesson Ferry Rd. (Highway 21); Hellmuth, Obata & Kassabaum, 1976

Four office modules, linked by a common-use core in sandblasted concrete with deeply recessed bronze windows. The precast double-T floor and roof system that supports long spans is expressed on the exterior. See color photograph, p. 19.

SC21. Maritz, Inc.

1355 North Highway Dr.; Raymond E. Maritz & Sons, 1980

This brick and structural-concrete complex is prominent on the north side of I-44, a short way east of Highway 141. It houses various business services—personnel motivation campaigns, audiovisual aids, consumer surveys, travel bookings. The Maritz architectural firm is separate.

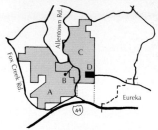

A. Rockwood Range
B. Greensfelder Memorial
C. Greensfelder Park
D. Camp Wyman

SC22. Greensfelder Memorial

West side of Allenton Rd.; Burks & Landberg, 1975

Memorial to Blanche and Albert Greensfelder, who bequeathed St. Louis County a large estate for a public park. On the site of the Greensfelder country home, destroyed by fire after the park was created. From the house's foundation stones the architects made a podium with benches. Monument in the middle, two offset halves of a cylindrical form, is of poured concrete.

153

10 North County

As St. Louis began to grow and prosper with the waning 18th century, farming became less attractive to most of its residents than commerce. Land prices rose and the ground was only moderately fruitful. For several reasons, farmers in the area looked beyond St. Louis for suitable land. French settlers on the east side of the river, apprehensive at France's cession of Illinois to England, were glad to find new opportunities in the friendlier political climate of Missouri.

Many found what they wanted north of St. Louis, along Coldwater Creek on the south side of the Missouri River. There was good prairie on the higher ground, and deep, rich bottomland. The bottoms were susceptible to flood, but more often than not would abundantly repay the farmer.

By 1785 French settlers established there had named their village Fleurissant, renamed St. Ferdinand in the Spanish regime, and made Florissant in 1939. The population grew to 185 by 1796, and to nearly 300 at the end of the century. West of that village, another farm community took root in 1794 and soon flourished. It was called then Marais des Liards, or "black-poplar marsh," and later took the name Bridgeton.

North County still sees a little farming, as well as great numbers of residential subdivisions and shopping centers. At the heart of North County is a monumental presence unlike anything else in the metropolitan area—McDonnell Douglas, its 38,000 employees busy in millions of square feet of factory, laboratory, and office space on the north side of the St. Louis airport. An architectural visit to North County should include a walk through Minoru Yamasaki's airport terminal (NC13) and a drive around the McDonnell Douglas tour de force that is still known locally as McAuto (NC11).

NC1. Gen. Daniel Bissell House

10225 Bellefontaine Rd.; 1814; Gerhardt Kramer, restoration

A two-story L-shaped brick house with a frame addition in the corner of the L; the addition is thought to have supplanted a stone building of c. 1812. The Bissell family continued to occupy the house until 1962 and made many modifications over a century and a half. Now the property of St. Louis County, restored and open as a museum.

NC2. Castle Park (formerly St. Vincent's Hospital)

1600 Castle Park Dr.; Eckel & Mann, Harvey Ellis, 1894; Henmi & Associates, renovation

A majestic former hospital on lines inspired by 17-century French chateaux has entered a new career as an apartment house. Careful renovation and remodeling saw to it that wrap-around parking lots were distanced visually by landscaping and that the 209 one- and two-bedroom units were attractively differentiated in plan. Two new entrances were built for easier access to parking from each part of the complex.

156

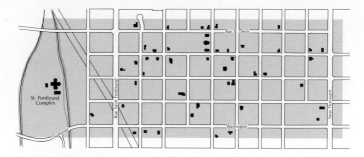

NC3. Florissant

The old-town district has 16 blocks with French street names, and house architecture reflecting building modes of its French, Spanish, and German settlers, as well as Eastern-seaboard types. The sampling offered here can be supplemented by maps and other materials obtainable at the City Hall and Visitors' Center.

NC4. Archambault House and outhouse

603 rue St. Denis; c. 1850; W. Philip Cotton, Jr., restoration

Built for Auguste Archambault, a French-Canadian "mountain man" who was a guide for John C. Frémont. Right-side front entrance, with interior halls to two rooms upstairs, two down. Fireplaces and mantels are original, as are the walls of the brick privy. Open. See also color photograph, p. 2.

NC5. Alvarez House

289 rue St. Denis; c. 1790

Probably the oldest building on the Missouri side of the St. Louis metro area, and the only one left from the Spanish regime. Eugenio Alvarez was the king's store-keeper. The front part of the house is original, with clapboards over vertical posts.

157

NC6. Aubuchon House

1002 rue St. Louis; c. 1800

Well-maintained board siding over horizontal logs. Auguste Aubuchon's house has been modified but preserves the Creole full-width veranda under a main roof that flattens its pitch on the way down from a lateral ridge.

NC7. Old St. Ferdinand Shrine

1 rue St. François; 1821, with spire and front wall of 1881; Gerhardt Kramer, preservation

Property of the Friends of Old St. Ferdinand. Father Pierre DeSmet, Jesuit missionary to western Indians, was ordained here, and the recently sainted Philippine Duchesne founded the first novitiate of the Society of the Sacred Heart on this site, as well as the first school for Indian girls in the United States.

NC8. Myers House

180 Dunn Rd.; c. 1869

Exceptionally fine detailing is seen in the two-story pedimented front porch with four sets of double columns. Original painted ceiling of 1886 in living room; the barn has a cupola and pedimented windows. Destruction of the John B. Myers House was averted by adjusting the planned route of I-270 in a way that proved to be more economical.

NC9. St. Stanislaus Museum of Jesuit History

700 Howdershell Rd.; 1840–1849

Until 1971 this was a unit of St. Stanislaus Seminary, the world's oldest Jesuit novitiate in continuous use, built of limestone quarried by the Jesuits. Father DeSmet's grave is among burials of priests in a small cemetery at rear. Other buildings are now owned by the Gateway College of Evangelism (Pentecostal).

NC10. Mallinckrodt Corporate Center

675 McDonnell Blvd.; Hellmuth, Obata & Kassabaum, 1977

Two buildings of warm-toned precast concrete, on the shore of a nine-acre lake, compose this chemical firm's headquarters. The main unit is built around two glazed and planted space frames as circulation cores. Pharmaceutical unit is long-span construction, with atrium spaces. See color photograph, p. 19.

NC11. McDonnell Douglas Information Services Co. (formerly McDonnell Automation Co., "McAuto")

North corner Lindbergh and McDonnell Blvds.; Hellmuth, Obata & Kassabaum, 1980, more units completed 1983

The high-tech look, enclosing more than a million square feet in a style made hospitable by landscaping and dramatic by the disposition of many geometrical blocks on various levels and axes. Color is used boldly, with expanses of blue-painted metal curtain wall articulating greater expanses of aluminum, and orange-red turning up as an accent in round air louvers and on the skin of tubular footbridges connecting the units. Flat black, white, mirror glass, and even glass block are used sparingly here and there, helping visitors orient themselves in a construction of great size and complexity. See color photograph, p. 20.

159

NC12. McDonnell Aircraft Engineering Campus

South corner Lindbergh and McDonnell Blvds.; Harris Armstrong, 1960

Three-building complex in which most of America's space vehicles were designed and built. The projecting mullions and ledges break the long, low facades into crisp patterns of light and shadow.

NC13. Main Terminal, Lambert–St. Louis International Airport

Entry from I-70; Hellmuth, Yamasaki & Leinweber, 1957, with Edgardo Contini and William C. E. Becker, structural engineers

Minoru Yamasaki's first "signature building," and one of few U.S. airport terminals to express the idea of flight on a monumental scale; two others of distinction are Dulles Airport and the TWA International Terminal at Kennedy Airport, both by Eero Saarinen. Yamasaki laid out a row of three groined concrete shells, each in the form of two intersecting shallow vaults, 32 feet high and 120 feet in span. The eight outward openings are glazed, and gussets are left open for skylights where the shells meet.

A fourth vault of identical design was added on the southeast end in 1965 by Hellmuth, Obata & Kassabaum, the firm that succeeded Hellmuth, Yamasaki & Leinweber while the terminal was under construction. HOK also designed the International Wing, 1976. The control tower, 1965, is one of several in the nation done to a design of I. M. Pei Associates. Concourses A, B, and C were redesigned to jet-age standards

by the firm of Berger-Field-Torno-Hurley. Sverdrup Corp. subsequently extended "C" concourse with the help of moving walkways and added an entire subterminal at the southeast end of a long new "D" concourse.

Parking garages on the southwest front have greatly diminished the view of the terminal from I-70, and the interior, which Yamasaki wanted to be open and airy, is cluttered with the ticketing facilities added by airlines to keep up with increased passenger traffic.

11 St. Charles

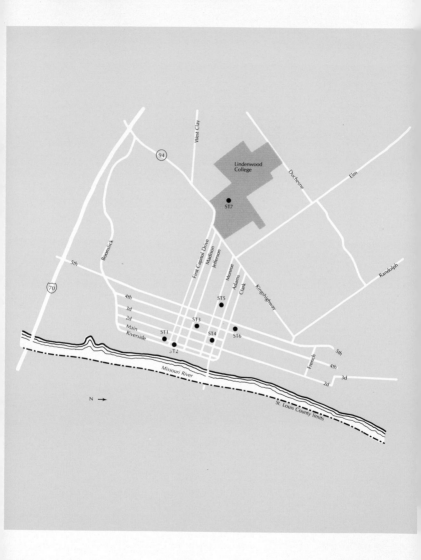

St. Charles as dealt with in this guide is not a region or even a city or town, but part of a small city—the 19th-century nucleus. The remains of early St. Charles are not as old as those of Ste. Genevieve or as grand as those of St. Louis, but they form pleasant, intact environments in which, for blocks on end, one can get a sense of the river town that preceded the rail and highway town.

Almost as soon as St. Louis took shape on the Mississippi riverfront, hunters noticed the abundance of game in the woods behind "les Petites Cotes"—the little shore, as it was called by its first French settlers in 1768. Farmers were drawn to the bottomland. At some point the prospering town took the name San Carlos. By 1800 it had 614 residents, more than twice as many as Florissant.

Then San Carlos was 20 miles or so northwest of St. Louis. Today St. Charles, even if it's a county seat on the other side of a wide river, is a St. Louis suburb. The mighty wave of development from the east has virtually filled a triangle bordered by I-70, Highway 61—40, and the Missouri River. The process was greatly accelerated by establishment in 1980 of a big General Motors assembly plant at Wentzville, near the west end of St. Charles County. In this context, St. Charles isn't on the fringe of St. Louis expansion, but halfway back to the Gateway Arch.

ST1. Main St.

St. Charles's Main St. preserves an unusually consistent stretch of early and middle 19th-century buildings. Some of them are illustrated here in a photograph, drawn plan, and drawn elevation.

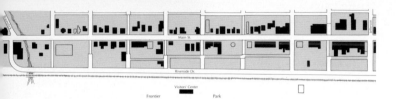

Visitors' Center

Frontier   Park

ST2. First Missouri Capitol

208–216 South Main St.; before 1821; restored by Kenneth Coombs, 1971

Of the four joined two-story brick buildings, the three at left housed on their second floor the governor's office and legislature from 1821 to 1826, when Missouri had just entered the Union. The lower building at right is of the same period but was apparently not part of the government center.

ST3. St. Charles County Courthouse

Third and Jefferson Sts.; Jerome B. Legg, 1903

Rusticated stone, round-arched windows, and cupola on a building of free neoclassical inspiration.

ST4. St. Charles County Justice Center

Block bounded by Second, Third, Adams, and Monroe Sts.; Powers Associates Inc., 1988

For a swiftly growing county in the west part of the St. Louis metropolitan area, a jail, juvenile court with cells, sheriff's department, police academy, and other law-enforcement facilities. In sharp contrast with the geometrical form and gold reflecting glass of the St. Charles Civic Center just two blocks away (William B. Ittner Inc., 1976), this 190,000-square-foot complex is tucked behind a four-story Second St. brick front that aims for a tone of 19th-century dignity and decorum.

ST5. St. Charles houses

Indeterminate of style and date, but looking at ease among hundreds of brick homes more or less like them. St. Charles's vernacular houses are a sight to see on a leisurely drive around the older parts of town; you don't often see chimneys penetrating dormers.

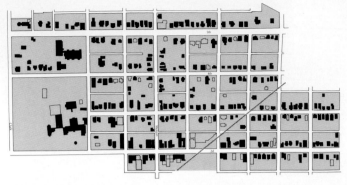

ST6. Frenchtown

The name isn't exact and may not even be old, but it suits a picturesque area along the west side of Second St., between Clark and French Sts., extending west to Fifth St. The houses are old and, although many don't look French, the photograph shows one that does.

ST7. Lindenwood College

The campus, at Kingshighway and Clay St., should be visited for the experience of its fine tree-lined entrance and the space created by buildings under the tree canopy. Building in foreground, Butler Hall (1915), and the nearly identical one just beyond, Ayres Hall, face east in a stately row. At far end can be seen the portico of Sibley Hall, the oldest on campus, with central part dating to 1857.

166

12 Outlying Missouri

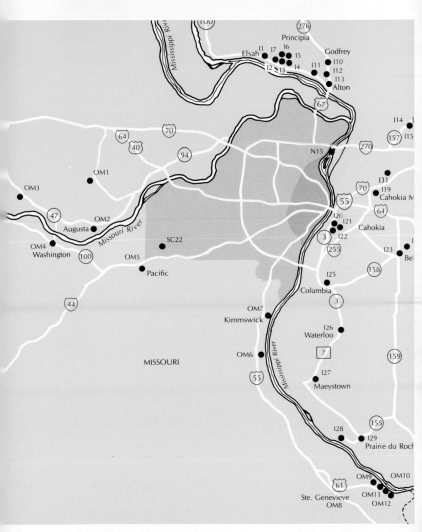

From the south part of the St. Louis metropolitan area, the drive to Ste. Genevieve is 50 miles, but I-55 makes it a quick as well as scenic trip, and the town is of unique importance in the upper Mississippi Valley for its concentration of French colonial buildings.

Explore the environs of Ste. Genevieve and you will find Zell, Bloomsdale, River aux Vases, St. Marys—attractions of a different order, later and more numerous than the French settlements, laid out in the mid-19th century by people who were mostly German. Their villages are found along the Mississippi and Missouri rivers in nearly every part of the state north of the Ohio River. In comparison with other 19th-century settlers, the Germans were more deliberate, more disposed to put down roots in their chosen ground.

Native Americans often speculated, took their profits, and moved on. The majority of Germans clearly aimed at re-creating in the New World the best aspects of the culture they had left behind. They built carefully, of brick and stone, to last and to look good.

A lot of their architectural *Gemütlichkeit* remains. You can see it along the Missouri River by following Highway 100 on the south bank, Highway 94 on the north—a favorite Sunday ride for motorists and bicyclists because of the loop opportunities afforded by bridges at Washington and Hermann.

Here, as in the Illinois section, we have included a couple of generalized pictures—a street in Augusta, a landscape with a country church—to suggest the pleasures of a leisurely ramble. If you visit Hannibal, set aside time for a return on Highway 79 along the Mississippi, with a look at Louisiana's imposing old city center, at Clarksville with its rare survival of a riverside street front, and at the scenic beauty of county roads south of Clarksville between the two main north-south highways.

OM1. Boone House

St. Charles County, Route F between New Melle and Highway 94; 1810

Built by Nathan Boone starting c. 1803. His father, Daniel Boone, lived here during his troubled old age, when old grants of land to him were repeatedly challenged, and died here in 1820, although the remains were supposedly reburied in Frankfort, Ky., 25 years later. Open.

OM2. Augusta

A 19th-century German town between Highway 94 and the Missouri River in the southwest corner of St. Charles County. Its comfortable accommodation to the verdant, hilly terrain is seen in many other villages along the river.

OM3. St. John's United Church of Christ

Four miles west of Treloar on Highway 94, in Warren County; 1870

This country church, with its parsonage and outbuildings, dozes at the edge of a strip of rich Missouri bottomland. The nearest village is Treloar (pop. 70).

OM4. Wehrmann House

212 Jefferson St., Washington; c. 1857

Brick pilasters and cornice give this house a monumental, even institutional look. First-floor window treatment suggests that the builder had too many door-width iron lintels on hand.

OM5. Gerald Harvath law office

221 North First St., Pacific; Ittner & Bowersox, 1983

Pointed-arch entries on both street fronts of this corner-lot building bring a note of Postmodern fashion to a quiet old town that was bypassed by I-44. Walls of red brick and tile, hip roof with its old-fashioned galvanized-iron look are deliberate evocations of the past.

OM6. Greystone

Bushberg Rd., near Pevely in Jefferson County; c. 1845

Intense, expressive Gothic Revival, with its profusion of steep-pitched gables and dormers, pointed arches, lacy bargeboards, and thicket of lancets and chimneys. A big rear porch overlooks the Mississippi River. Not accessible.

170

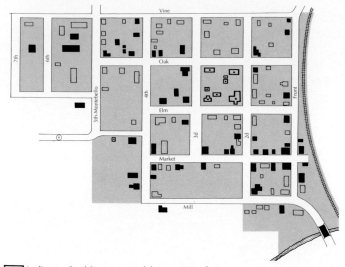

[•] indicates buildings moved from original sites

OM7. Kimmswick

Early settlement on the Mississippi, in Jefferson County, is reachable from Highway 61, and there is a marked exit on I-55. A number of interesting 19th-century buildings have survived in place, like the half-timber Herrmann-Oheim House that was begun in 1859. Others, including the double log house in the photo, have been removed from sites where they were threatened and reerected in Kimmswick on the initiative of a local resident, Mrs. Lucianna Gladney Ross.

The settlement was started before 1800 by Thomas Jones, who at first sold salt from nearby deposits, then developed a spa on Rock Creek that he called Crystal Springs or Montesano; excursion boats brought St. Louisans to the summer resort. In 1857 the St. Louis and Iron Mountain (later Missouri Pacific) Railroad came through en route to mines in the hills to the southwest, and Theodore Kimm subdivided the old resort property to create the village of Kimmswick.

171

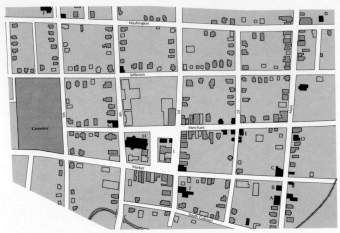

A. Louis Bolduc House; B. Rene Lemeillure House; C. Jean Baptiste Vallé House; D. Vital Ste. Gemme Beauvais House; E. Felix Vallé State Historic Site; F. Ste. Genevieve Academy; G. Guibord-Valle House; H. Church of Ste. Genevieve; I. Town Square

OM8. Ste. Genevieve

Ste. Genevieve was founded at an uncertain date in the mid-18th century; its first importance was as a river port for lead from mines in the vicinity of Mine la Motte, deep in the hills southwest of the town. A flood in 1785 caused the townspeople to move back from the riverbank to the present foothill site. Its present importance is great as a treasury of Creole culture in the Mississippi Valley, with many buildings remaining from the late 18th and early 19th century. Dates given for buildings in the following Ste. Genevieve entries have been recently established by University of Missouri laboratory analysis of tree ring patterns in sample wood borings. They are later than the dates assigned by local tradition.

OM9. Jean Baptiste Vallé House

Main & Market Sts., Ste. Genevieve; c. 1794

Vallé was the last commandant of the town after it came under U.S. jurisdiction. Part of the stone foundation reaches four-foot thickness, possibly for use as a fortress. The house has been modified but retains its early character. Private.

172

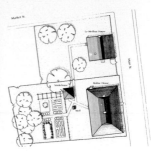

OM10. Bolduc House

125 South Main St., Ste. Genevieve; c. 1793

Meticulously restored. Exterior photograph shows the back of the house with a kitchen that interrupts a wrap-around porch. Walls are oak posts on a stone foundation, the vertical gaps closed with a mixture of clay and straw. A museum house, open.

OM11. Felix Vallé House

Second & Merchant Sts., Ste. Genevieve; 1818; William Bodley Lane, restoration

Traditions mix here, with a two-pitched Creole roof in back, Georgian window treatment and cornice dentils in front. Open.

173

OM12. Bequet-Ribault House

West side of St. Marys Road, 1/2 mile south of South Gabouri Creek; c. 1808

Best example in Ste. Genevieve of *poteaux en terre* construction, with walls of close-spaced vertical logs—in this case, red cedar—planted in a trench. The cracks were filled with clay-and-straw mud and the walls then whitewashed. Scrupulously restored and open as a museum house.

13 Illinois

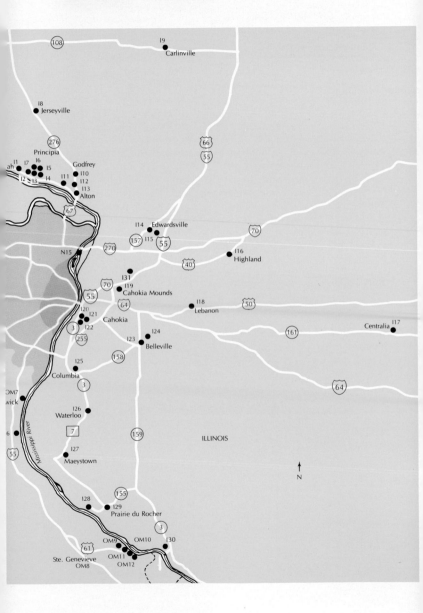

Because of greatly varying road and traffic conditions, a St. Louis-based architectural tour into Illinois can't reasonably be confined to a given radius. This guidebook accordingly points to some things that may be seen in an easy one-day excursion from any starting point in St. Louis.

Elsah, Principia College (where a campus tour must be prearranged; see I2), and Alton, with its splendid old blufftop residential suburb called Fairmount, are ample for a long day's runout. Carlinville with its courthouse is twice as many miles from St. Louis, but since most of the miles are on interstate highways, it's a quick trip. In fact, anyone going that far in the direction of Springfield, Ill., might well want to go the rest of the way to see Frank Lloyd Wright's sumptuous Dana-Thomas House of 1904, with most of its Wright-designed furnishings intact. It's outside the St. Louis metropolitan area, but the driving time on I-55 is no more than an hour and a half.

Our eastern boundary touches Centralia, for the sake of a 1941 International style house that was still being cared for in 1988 by its appreciative original owners. On the south, we go almost to Chester for a look at the Pierre Menard house.

Just as in Missouri, visitors exploring on their own will find that 19th-century settlers, particularly Germans, endowed their land liberally and enduringly with attractive buildings. They are quite numerous, and they constitute collective architectural experiences or environments more than individual sights.

Photos of Waterloo and Maeystown in this book endeavor, not very successfully, to suggest that experience. A leisurely drive will make the point in Waterloo, Maeystown, and many other old towns and cities, including Freeburg, Sparta, Red Bud, St. Libory, Grafton, Belleville, Chester, and Quincy.

I1. Elsah

Street elevation and photograph show houses along the village's main street. Elsah lies at the mouth of a narrow valley that breaks the line of bluffs confronting the Mississippi. The man who owned the valley, James Semple, laid out a town in 1853, with a flour mill and distillery at the river landing; he counted on the easy road between river and upland wheat farms to bring money to his settlement. Elsah prospered moderately but did not grow further, so its first-generation houses, about 50 of them put up in the late 1850s, survived with few losses into the 20th century. Principia College, which in 1931 became the largest landowner in the region, has taken care from the beginning to preserve the little river village as much as possible from the attentions of developers. About 55 percent of Elsah's houses are owned by Principia College and its friends. The campus holdings on both sides of Elsah total about 3,600 acres.

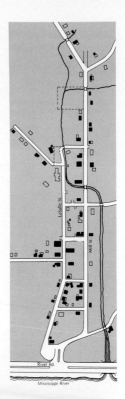

Mississippi River

177

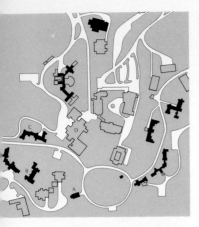

A. Chapel; B. Howard House; C. Anderson Hall; D. Howard Center; buildings by Maybeck are indicated by solid black.

12. Principia College

In 1898, when Christian Science as a religion was only 19 years old, its St. Louis congregation founded a grammar school at 4484–86 Enright Ave. A junior college was added in 1912. Ten years later, the congregation was looking ahead to a four-year college and northwestward for a suitable campus.

In 1930 they found a 300-acre site around a lake in St. Louis County and engaged Bernard Maybeck, a San Francisco–based architect admired for his design of a Christian Science church in Berkeley, California, to prepare a comprehensive campus design. When it was discovered that a major north-south artery was planned nearby and that sewer connections would be costly, the church began looking for another site.

One possibility was the heights overlooking the Mississippi River near Elsah, Illinois. The school's late art instructor, Frederick Oakes Sylvester, had bought a summer cabin above Elsah and introduced many of his colleagues and students to the beauties of the place.

Three blufftop tracts totaling 2,200 acres had just come on the market and could be bought cheap. Maybeck was delighted at the superior quality and extent offered by the Elsah purchase, so he went back to the drawing board with enthusiasm. Principia College moved to its new home in 1935. Visits to the Elsah campus may be arranged by phoning (618) 374-2131. The lower school has its own suburban campus at 13201 Clayton Rd. in St. Louis County.

13. Principia College Chapel

On the Elsah campus; Bernard Maybeck, 1934

The prevailing style of Maybeck's Principia buildings is Tudor, but his chapel is New England Colonial, because the student body wanted it that way. The structure is reinforced concrete faced with limestone. Near the bluffside chapel is a little experimental building that Principia has preserved in Maybeck's memory. The architect used "Mistake House" to test unusual materials and techniques that he wanted to employ on the main campus.

178

I4. Howard House

On Principia's Elsah campus; Bernard Maybeck, 1934

This and three other dormitories exemplify the look of an English village that the architect wanted for his blufftop campus. Varicolored roof tiles are arranged in artfully irregular patterns that concentrate darker hues near the eaves. See color photograph, p. 17.

I5. Anderson House

On Principia's Elsah campus; Bernard Maybeck, 1934

First-floor dormitory parlor, with arched roof trusses in reinforced concrete. Maybeck's Principia buildings combine an appearance of picturesque age with an extraordinarily robust modern structural system, designed to resist earthquakes as well as ordinary wear and tear.

I6. Howard Center

On Principia's Elsah campus; Smith-Entzeroth, 1968

Tile roofs, rough concrete lintels, and soft hand-molded brick harmonize with the Maybeck buildings, while forms belong to the 20th century. Howard is a student center, similar in design to two women's dormitories by Smith-Entzeroth, completed in 1966 and 1969.

179

17. Eliestoun

On Principia's Elsah campus; Longfellow, Alden & Harlow, 1890

Shingled house was built for the owner of a choice blufftop tract southeast of the main campus. Alexander Wadsworth Longfellow had worked in the office of H. H. Richardson and was a nephew of Henry Wadsworth Longfellow. Some of the original shingles are a cement-asbestos composition.

18. Jersey County Courthouse

Jerseyville public square; Henry Elliott, 1894

Richardsonian Romanesque, with increasingly free variations on the way to the summit.

19. Macoupin County Courthouse

In central Carlinville; E. E. Meyers, 1870

Eclectic neoclassicism with a Renaissance dome surmounting deep pediments, entablature with dentils and brackets, and a large Corinthian order on columns and pilasters. The high courtrooms on the second floor have tall Romanesque windows rising into the Corinthian foliage.

I10. Godfrey Christian Church

Highway 67, Godfrey; 1854

Benjamin Godfrey, a retired sea captain, founded Monticello College (now Lewis & Clark Junior College) across the road from his home. This frame building in the New England style was the college's chapel and a community church. Extensively restored in 1939.

I11. Levis House

70 Danforth St. Rd., Alton; Study, Farrar & Majers, 1925

Outstanding among the many fine houses in Alton's blufftop Fairmount district is this evocation in stone of 16th-century England, restrained in ornament, making its effect through artful disposition of masses and openings.

I12. Haskell Playhouse

1211 Henry St., Alton; c. 1885

Built in their backyard by Dr. and Mrs. William A. Haskell for their daughter Ruth, who died of a childhood disease in 1889. The residence now at the address is newer.

181

I13. Lyman Trumbull House

1105 Henry St., Alton; c. 1820

Trumbull (1813–1896) bought and renovated this handsome Federal style house in 1849 when he was a justice of the Illinois Supreme Court. As a U.S. senator (1855–1873) he moved from the Democratic to the Republican party and was chairman of the judiciary committee that advanced the 13th amendment to the U.S. Constitution, abolishing slavery.

I14. Southern Illinois University, Edwardsville campus

West of Edwardsville; Hellmuth, Obata & Kassabaum, with Sasaki, Walker & Associates, landscaping, 1965

Brick, precast concrete panels, and glass are set out in strong geometric compositions over a spacious campus. SIU is custodian of an important collection of Louis Sullivan architectural ornament assembled by the late Richard Nickel of Chicago; a part of it is permanently displayed in Lovejoy Library on the campus. The piece illustrated here is a sconce from the Wainwright Building.

182

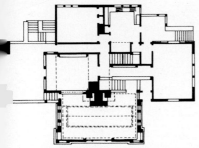

I15. Griffin House

705 St. Louis Ave., Edwardsville; Walter Burley Griffin, 1910

Low-pitched roof with deep over-hangs, massive central chimney, and horizontal emphases, including casement windows in bands, mark this as a product of the "Prairie School" of architects influenced by Frank Lloyd Wright around the turn of the century. Walter Burley Griffin, a successful alumnus of Wright's Oak Park studio, designed this home for a relative.

I16. Latzer Library

In central Highland; Helfensteller, Hirsch & Watson, 1929

Exuberant neo-Palladian building presents big front windows and a round entry arch that rises through the roofline. Building, books to stock it, and an endowment fund were given to the town of Highland as a memorial by the family of Louis Latzer, one of the founders of the Helvetia Condensing Co., which grew from its Highland beginning into the giant Pet Inc. The library has had two additions and now contains more than 30,000 bound volumes.

183

I17. J. Paul Allen House

16 Orchard Drive, Centralia; Diedrich Rixmann, 1941

Extremely rare instance of an International Style residence completed before World War II. The original owners continued to occupy the house in mid-1988; their only significant alteration has been to apply vertical metal siding over the architect's vertical redwood siding, which was disfigured by weathering and raised grain. Rixmann at the time was a young graduate and admired the work of Walter Gropius.

I18. McKendree College Chapel

On the campus at Lebanon; 1857

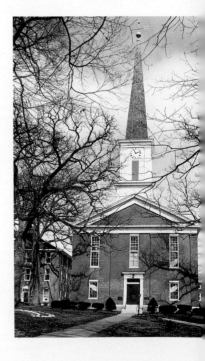

The steeple began to vibrate alarmingly when its bells rang the hour, so safety-conscious school officials contacted a St. Louis architectural firm, which advised them to pull down the tower immediately. It was done, in 1959, but outrage among alumni and friends of the old chapel was such that money was soon raised for reconstruction. Gerhardt Kramer supervised building of the new steeple (using Historic American Buildings Survey measurements of the old one) and a general restoration of the building.

184

I19. Cahokia Mounds Historic Site

On Collinsville Rd. (old Highway 40) south of I-70, between Exits 6 and 9. Visitors leaving I-70 on Exit 6 (Highway 111) turn east on Collinsville Rd.; if Exit 9 (Black Lane) is used, turn west on Collinsville Rd.

The biggest mound, 100 feet high and covering 14 acres with its base, looms close to I-70. Cahokia Indians built their earthworks over many years in the era corresponding to Europe's Middle Ages. Their descendants could not explain the purpose of the mounds to European explorers, and many aspects of these remarkable constructions remain obscure. A small museum with artifacts and conjectural restorations of the Indians' culture is being replaced by a $6 million, 33,000-square-foot building (rendering above) for the proper display of all that archaeology has revealed on the mound site. In mid-1988 construction of the new museum was far advanced, and it was expected to open in spring 1989. Design is by Architectural Associates Inc. of Collinsville.

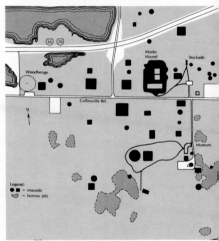

I20. Church of the Holy Family

Highways 3 and 157, Cahokia; 1797. (The city of Cahokia is 14 miles southwest of Cahokia Mounds [I19] via I-255.)

One of the oldest buildings in the Mississippi Valley and probably the oldest church, yet the Cahokia settlement is almost a century older; Father St. Cosme, of the Jesuit Seminary of Quebec, founded the mission of the Holy Family in 1699 with a small wood church on or near this site. A second church was built in 1737 but fell derelict when English forces expelled the Jesuits in 1763. The present church was built partly from sal-

185

vage materials left on the site, including remains of the rectory.

Walls are of walnut logs, squared on the faces and channeled on the sides to hold a fill of mortar and rubble masonry. They are placed vertically in the French fashion and lean inward about 5 inches at the top. The roof trusses we see now were hidden by a board ceiling, and horizontal lap siding was nailed over the log walls long ago; it was removed in a restoration completed in 1950. The low lateral bay at the rear was added in 1833 to accommodate a sacristy, organ, and choir.

The Cahokia Courthouse (I21) and Jarrot House (I22) are an easy walk from the church.

I21. Cahokia Courthouse

Cahokia; c. 1737

Much restored and worked over, but some of its elements still belong to the oldest building in the Midwest. It was built as a home by Capt. Jean-Baptiste Saucier, who laid out Fort de Chartres. His son sold it in 1793 to St. Clair County for a courthouse. It was installed at the St. Louis World's Fair of 1904, and later in Chicago's Jackson Park. The remains were sent back to Cahokia in 1939 for reconstruction as a state memorial. Open.

122. Jarrot House

Cahokia; 1798, 1806

The oldest brick building in Illinois is of late Colonial style, with two stories and attic. Handmade brick with black headers, but not in regular patterns. Lafayette is said to have danced in the second-floor ballroom, whose floor is worn down around the knots in the wood. Open.

123. St. Peter Cathedral

West Harrison and South Third Sts., Belleville; 1863, with major additions by Paul J. Saunders, 1955–1969

The old Gothic Revival parish church was damaged by fire and repaired in 1912 by Victor J. Klutho. Remodeling undertaken in 1955 involved extending the nave into the former rectory site (background in photograph) and complete redecoration of the interior.

124. Dobschutz House

701 East Washington St., Belleville; 1866

Fluently detailed roof brackets, window lintels, railings, and trim for the bull's-eye attic window embellish this shapely elaboration on a Georgian theme. All that detail is cast iron, from a town that was the stovemaking capital of the Midwest.

187

125. Grosse House

625 N. Main St., Columbia; John Grundlach, builder, c. 1858

The owner, A. Grosse, had a tavern and was part owner of a brewery. The sawtooth corbel pattern in the brick, iron lintels, and a pair of little columns inserted in the entry make this a memorable facade.

126. Square at Waterloo

Mid-19th-century Federal style brick buildings are plentiful in Illinois, with an especially pleasant concentration around the courthouse in Waterloo.

127. Maeystown

A farm village of 1852, 9 miles southwest of Waterloo. Stone houses, a stone-bridged brook, and tranquillity, set in countryside of great beauty.

188

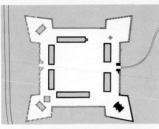

128. Fort de Chartres

Near Prairie du Rocher;
Jean-Baptiste Saucier, 1756

The last French outpost in Louisiana, established as part of a chain of fortifications from Quebec to New Orleans, was a walled enclosure of about 10 buildings for 400 soldiers. The powder magazine with its vaulted stone roof remained intact; the gatehouse and several barracks units have been reconstructed from ruins and foundations.

129. Creole house

Prairie du Rocher; c. 1800

One of the few structures remaining from the early days of an old French village. It has passed to the Randolph County Historical Society for conservation.

189

130. Menard House

River road north of Chester; 1802

Pierre Menard ran a trading post at nearby Kaskaskia, the second white settlement in Illinois; a change of course by the Mississippi long afterward cut off the house from Kaskaskia, which can now only be reached by land from Missouri. A veranda rambles genially around the house on unequally spaced piers. Studs in the house walls are mortised and tenoned into sills, while roof trusses are secured by wood pins, all hand-hewn. Meticulously restored and open.

131. Illinois State Building

North side of I-70 between I-255 and Highway 157 interchanges, Collinsville; Architectural Associates Inc., 1987

Geometrical patterning of dark-brown against buff brick, deeply recessed window ribbons of dark reflective glass, placement of squared over rounded corners, and sculptural treatment of brick curtain wall are elements in a complex but harmonious design. They make this regional state office building stand out authoritatively in its Postmodern commercial environment along a frontage road. Two above-grade levels enclose 155,000 square feet.

190

Some Old Vernacular House Types

On the pages that follow are drawings of 16 house fronts and of one neighborhood store with living quarters above. Addresses are not given here because the point is to illustrate some vernacular *types* on the lower-income and middle-income St. Louis housing market. The dates are mostly in the last half of the 19th century, with a couple of examples at the end from around 1910. Most are found in the near north and south sides of the city.

The wall material of overwhelming preference was brick, resting on a stone foundation, with a slate roof, or perhaps a slated mansard masking a built-up flat roof. Decorative elements would range from a corbeled shallow cornice and arched window lintels, in the thriftier models, to window and door trims in stone or terra-cotta, engaged columns in cast iron, wrought-iron roof cresting, and ornamental moldings in sheet copper or iron.

In no case is an architect's name attached, as far as we know. Builders usually laid out housing of this kind by freely adapting a design seen in a plan book, or in the next block over. An experienced builder would play a set of variations on a few well-tried themes, adjusting his measurements to fit the lot, his ornaments according to what was currently available from suppliers at a good price.

Regular spacing of openings and simple lintels show some Greek Revival influence.

191

Cast-iron ornamental lintels above openings are the main decorative elements of this double house, showing the influence of the Renaissance Revival.

Flounder: long, narrow house with roof pitched to one side.

Brick parapets, double chimneys, and brick cornice are main features of this double house type.

Two-story variation of the preceding house.

Tall narrow windows accent the verticality of this French-influenced mansard type.

Characteristic corner store with dwelling above. Inventive dormer designs ornament the mansard roof.

Ornamental iron cresting, patterned slate on mansard roof, brick and terra-cotta cornice, and rusticated base show influence of the French Second Empire style. Entrance is at side.

Stylized arch over second-floor window, dormer, and other arches show influence of Eastlake and Queen Anne styles.

Rusticated basement, wide, articulated arches on first-story windows, and shaped dormers show the influence of Richardsonian Romanesque style.

Rusticated base, wide brick arches, brick projection under gable windows, and asymmetrical composition define this type as Richardsonian Romanesque.

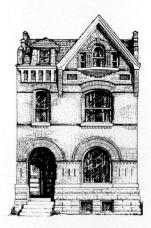

Arches, corbeled parapet, and pediment enrich a simple box with a flat roof.

Much of the architectural interest of this flat-roof type is due to the garlanded cornice, the varied skyline, and the sheet-metal flower on the gable.

The varied brick, terra-cotta, and stone details enrich a simple shape.

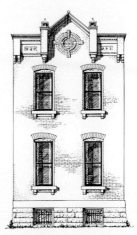

The Broken Frieze (where second-floor windows notch into the frieze) is a type that may be unique to St. Louis.

Two-story St. Louis masonry version of the California Bungalow style.

St. Louis version of Arts & Crafts style with some Spanish flavor in brick and tile.

196

Bibliography

Bryan, John Albury. *Missouri's Contribution to American Architecture*. St. Louis: St. Louis Architectural Club, 1928.

Cotton, W. Philip, Jr. *100 Historic Buildings in St. Louis County*. Clayton, Mo.: St. Louis County Department of Parks and Recreation, 1970.

Faherty, William Barnaby, S.J. *Henry Shaw: His Life and Legacies*. Columbia: University of Missouri Press, 1987.

Hunter, Julius K. *Kingsbury Place: The First Two Hundred Years*. St. Louis: C. V. Mosby Co., 1982.

————. *Westmoreland and Portland Places: The History and Architecture of America's Premier Private Streets, 1888–1988*. Columbia: University of Missouri Press, 1988.

Loughlin, Caroline, and Catherine Anderson. *Forest Park*. Columbia: University of Missouri Press, 1986.

Lowic, Lawrence. *The Architectural Heritage of St. Louis, 1803–1891*. St. Louis: Washington University Gallery of Art, 1982.

McCue, George. *The Building Art in St. Louis: Two Centuries*. 3d ed. rev. St. Louis: St. Louis Chapter of the American Institute of Architects Foundation, 1981.

Musick, James B. *St. Louis as a Fortified Town*. St. Louis: R. F. Miller Press, 1941.

Parkview Book Committee. *Urban Oasis: 75 Years in Parkview*. St. Louis: Boar's Head Press, 1979.

Peterson, Charles E. *Colonial St. Louis: Building a Creole Capital*. St. Louis: Missouri Historical Society, 1949.

Pickens, Buford, and Margaretta J. Darnall. *Washington University in St. Louis: Its Design and Architecture*. St. Louis: Washington University School of Architecture, Gallery of Art, 1978.

Powell, Mary. *Public Art in St. Louis*. 2d ed. rev. St. Louis: St. Louis Public Library Monthly Bulletin, July-August 1925.

Primm, James Neal. *Lion of the Valley: St. Louis, Missouri*. Boulder: Pruett Publishing Co., 1981.

Randall, John D. *The Art of Office Buildings: Sullivan's Wainwright and the St. Louis Real Estate Boom*. Springfield, Ill.: John D. Randall, 1972.

St. Louis County Historic Buildings Commission. *Historic Buildings in St. Louis County*. Clayton, Mo.: St. Louis County Department of Parks and Recreation, 1983.

Savage, Charles C. *Architecture of the Private Streets of St. Louis: The Architects and the Houses They Designed*. Columbia: University of Missouri Press, 1987.

Toft, Carolyn H., and Jane M. Porter. *Compton Heights*. St. Louis: Landmarks Association of St. Louis, 1984.

Troen, Selwyn K., and Glen E. Holt, eds. *St. Louis*. New York: New Viewpoints (Franklin Watts), 1977.

Writers' Program of Works Progress Administration. *Missouri: A Guide to the Show-Me State*. American Guide Series. New York: Duell, Sloan and Pearce, 1941. Rpt. as *The WPA Guide to 1930s Missouri*. Lawrence: University Press of Kansas, 1986.

Index

(Page numbers in italics refer to color illustrations)

Because of personnel changes or succession, the names of some architectural firms now differ from the identifications attached to their work of past years. Architectural offices are indexed in this guide according to their name style at the time of each listed project. For a summary of offices with modified names, but with maintained continuity, see page 209, immediately following this index.

199

201

204

206

207

Architectural Firm Name Changes

Previous Name or Names	Current Name
Bernoudy, Mutrux & Bauer	Bernoudy & Associates
Hellmuth, Yamasaki & Leinweber	Hellmuth, Obata & Kassabaum
Hoffmann/Saur & Associates	Louis R. Saur & Associates
Murphy & Mackey	Murphy, Downey, Wofford & Richman
Peckham-Guyton	Peckham Guyton Albers & Viets
Shepley, Rutan & Coolidge; Mauran, Russell & Garden; Mauran, Russell & Crowell; Russell, Mullgardt, Schwarz, Van Hoefen; Schwarz & Van Hoefen; Schwarz & Henmi; Henmi, Zobel & Fott; Henmi Jen Enderling	Henmi & Associates

Illustration Credits

(Page numbers in italics refer to color illustrations)

Anthony J. Amato, Jr.: D11 plan, NS7 section

Architectural Associates: I31

Arteaga Photos: pp. *10–11 (D50)*, N2, N2 interior, N12, N14

Pat Hays Baer: pp. xx, 26–27, 28, 29, 60, 68, 82, 90, 100, 114, 122, 126, 134, 143, 154, 162, 167, 175, 191–96, and D1 plan, D5 plan, D11 section, D12, M3 plan, W8, W9 plan, W9 elevation, W20, W23, W35 plan, W39 plan, W42 plan, NS12, NS13, NS16, NS19 plan, S1 plan, S3, S4, S12, S21, S24, N3, N4 plan, N6, N10, N11 plan, UC1 plan, UC5 plan, UC12 plan, UC13 plan, SC2, SC9 plan, SC12 plan, SC17 plan, SC18 plan, SC22 plan, NC3, ST1 plan, ST1 elevation, ST6 plan, ST7 plan, OM7 plan, OM8, I1 plan, I2 plan, I15 plan, I19 plan, I28 plan

Richard Bliss: D14, D24 bottom, D28, D42, D44 bottom right, D45, D46, D51, D52, D53 exterior, D56, M1, M6, M7, M11, M12 exterior, W5 exterior, W6, W13-14-15-16, W17, W19, W24, W36, W37, W41, W43, W45, NS2, NS3, NS6, NS8, NS17 exterior, NS19, NS21, S13, S14, S16, S19, S22, S26, S28, UC5, UC6 left, UC7, UC12 left, WC17, SC5, SC10, SC12, SC13, SC15, SC16, SC18, NC8, OM1, OM7 left, OM9, OM10 exterior, OM11, I10, I30

Booker Associates: I19

W. Philip Cotton, Jr.: pp. 2 *(NC4)*, 3 *(S15)*, 7 *(N13)*, 14 bottom, 15 top left, 15 top right, 15 center, 15 bottom, 16 *(M12)*, 17 *(I4)*, 17 *(D51)*, and D5, D7, D9 lower, D11 bottom right, D22, D24 top left, D24 top right, D25, D27 lower, D30, D31, D32, D40, D48, D50 bottom left, W4, W11, W12, W38, NS7 left, NS7 right, NS11, NS14, NS15, NS20, NS22, S1, S9, S11, S17, S23, S27, N1, N4 top, N4 bottom, N11, N13 bottom, UC3, UC6 right, UC9, UC10, UC19, WC5, WC10, SC3, SC4, SC6, SC7, SC11, NC1, NC4, NC5, NC6, NC7, NC9, ST1, ST3, ST5, ST6, ST7, OM2, OM3, OM7 right, OM10 interior, I11, I13, I17, I18, I21, I28 lower, I29

Exhibition of the German Empire, Official Catalog (Berlin, 1904): p. xxvii

Sam Fentress: pp. *22 (D17), 23 (D37)*, and D16, D18, D33, D36, D50, WC3

Richard Finke: M3 interior

French Government Tourist Office: D44 bottom left

Mary Henderson Gass: D24 elevation diagram, D29 plan, D53 plan, W5 plan, W5 section

General American Life Insurance Co.: p. *19 (SC20)*

Hellmuth, Obata & Kassabaum: pp. xxx, *1 (D1 and D11)*, and D26, NC13, NC13 interior

Hedrich-Blessing, photographer: WC7, I14

Balthazar Korab, photographer: NS1

Barbara Elliott Martin, photographer: D10

William Mathis, photographer: p. 9 *(D50)* and D50 center, S7, WC18

Kiku Obata, photographer: W44, WC9

Robert Pettus, photographer: p. *24 (D19)* and WC13

George Silk, photographer: pp. *18 (WC12), 20 (NC11)*, and WC12 exterior

Henmi & Assoc., Inc.: NC2

Historic American Buildings Survey, National Park Service

Jack E. Boucher, photographer: pp. xiv, *4 (N8), 4 (N7), 5 (NS18), 9 (W26)*, 21

210

(D49), and D1, D53 center right, N13 upper, OM12

Paul Piaget, photographer: M10

Illinois Department of Transportation: SC1

Illinois Historic Preservation Agency: I8

Wm. B. Ittner, Inc.: D47, W32, S2, N5

Bruce Jager: SC8

Maurice Johansen: D21, UC14, SC14, ST2

Gerhardt Kramer: OM6, I12

Kurt Landberg: UC13

Christopher Lark: WC15

Roberta Lawrence: D4, W28, W29, W30, N9

Ted McCrea: D6

George McCue: p. xxxi

McDonnell Douglas: NC12

Eric Mack: I1 elevation

Daniel T. Magidson: M2

Maritz, Inc.: SC21

Barbara Elliott Martin: D15, D34, W46

James Mellow: D57

Missouri Botanical Garden: S5, S6, S8, S10

Missouri Historical Society: pp. xviii, xix, xxii, xxiii, and D27 top, W5 interior, W27, W34

Mac Mizuki: W3

Monsanto Company: WC6

Murphy, Downey, Wofford & Richman: p. *18 (S5)* and W1, W2, W39, S20 exterior, S20 interior

James B. Musick, *St. Louis as a Fortified Town* (St. Louis: R. F. Miller Press, 1941): p. xvii

John Wm. Nagel: pp. *16 (M9), 17 (WC11),* and D3 bottom left, M3 exterior, M13

Nooney Company: UC20

Osmund Overby: OM10 plan

Frank Peters: WC4

Robert Pettus: pp. *3 (D57), 2–3 (D3), 6 (D24 bottom), 7 (D24 top), 12 (NS17), 14 (W31), 19 (NC10), 21 (WC14), 23 (WC16),* and D2, D8, D23, D29 exterior, D29 interior, D35, D38, D39, D44 top, D44 interior, D53 interior, D54 exterior, D54 interior, D55, W21, N15, UC2 exterior, UC2 interior, UC12 interior, UC15, UC16, WC2, OM5, I20 exterior, I20 interior, I23

Doug Pierce: W40, NS4, NS10, S25, OM4

Doug Pierce and Steve Downen: I9, I15, I16, I22, I24, I25, I26, I27, I28 top

Powers Associates: ST4

Principia College: I1 center, I3, I5, I6, I7

Cervin Robinson: p. 6 *(D24 top)*

The Saint Louis Art Museum, Robert Pettus, photographer: W35 exterior, W35 interior

St. Louis County Department of Parks and Recreation: UC1 lower, SC9 left, SC19, SC22 upper

St. Louis Union Station: D50 elevation

Louis R. Saur & Associates, Robert Pettus, photographer: WC8

Martin Schweig Studio: NS9

Bryan Sechrist: M4, M5, M8, W7, W10, W18, S18

Jerry Seegers: W42

SMP/Smith-Entzeroth: UC17, UC18, SC17

Walter B. Stevens, *History of St. Louis, the Fourth City 1864–1909, Vol. I* (St. Louis–Chicago: S. G. Clarke Publishing Co., 1909): D44 center left

Sverdrup Corporation: D9 upper, D18 plan

Swekosky Photo Collection, School Sisters of Notre Dame, St. Louis: W22

Team Four, Inc.: D13

The University Museum, Southern Illinois University at Edwardsville: I14 bottom

University of Missouri Press: W25

James Van Horn: D20

Ralph Eglin Wafer: D41, D43, WC1

The Wainwright Building (rental brochure, ca. 1892): D24 rendering

Washington University student (unidentified): NS5 elevation

Wedemeyer Cernik Corrubia: M12 section

Herb Weitman, Washington University in St. Louis: p. *13 (UC6)* and UC8, UC11

Calvin W. Woodward, *History of the St. Louis Bridge* (St. Louis, 1881): D3 elevation, D3 bottom right

Jack Zehrt: pp. *8 (NS7), 13 (W5)*

Peter Zimmerman: W47

211

Obligations

Reference and consultation:
Esley Hamilton, St. Louis County Department of Parks and Recreation; the late Martha Hilligoss, St. Louis Public Library; Charles B. Hosmer, Jr., Principia College; Osmund Overby, University of Missouri–Columbia; Shannon Paul, St. Louis Public Library; Keith Sculle, Illinois Historic Preservation Agency; Duane Sneddeker, Missouri Historical Society

Photo printing by Silver Image.